I Guess I'll Get The Papers And Go Home

The Life Of Doc Cheatham

by

Adolphus "Doc" Cheatham

Edited by
Alyn Shipton

Recording Chronology by
Howard Rye

CASSELL

London and Washington

Cassell
Wellington House, 125 Strand, London, WC2R 0BB
PO Box 605, Herndon, VA 20172, USA

First published 1995 in a limited handbound edition of five copies
by Bayou Press Ltd, Wheatley, Oxford

This edition first published 1996 in hardback in Great Britain by
Cassell plc by arrangement with Bayou Press Ltd

First paperback edition 1998

British Library Cataloguing-in-Publication Data
A catalogue record for this book is available from the British Library

ISBN 0 304 33611 4 (hardback)
    0 304 70316 8 (paperback)

Library of Congress Cataloging-in-Publication Data
Cheatham, Doc.
   I guess I'll get the papers and go home: the life of Doc Cheatham
/by Adolphus "Doc" Cheatham; edited by Alyn Shipton; recording
chronology by Howard Rye.–1st pbk. ed.
     p. cm.
   "First published 1995 in a limited handbound edition of five
copies by Bayou Press Ltd., Wheatley, Oxford"–T.p. verso.
   "Recording chronology": p.
   Includes bibliographical references (p.   ) and index.
   ISBN 0-304-70316-8 (pb)
   1. Cheatham, Doc. 2. Jazz musicians–United States–Biography.
I. Shipton, Alyn. II. Rye, Howard. III. Title.
ML419.C48A3 1998
781.65'092–dc21
[B]   97-49640
                                                       CIP
                                                       MN

Typeset by Oompah Books, Wheatley
Printed and bound in Great Britain by Biddles Ltd, Guildford and King's Lynn

Contents

Editor's Note
and Acknowledgements

Doc Cheatham came to Europe in 1988 with Lars Edegran's band from New Orleans. Also playing in that band was my old friend and colleague saxophonist Bill Greenow, who told me that Doc was working on an autobiography, and would welcome my advice. We met in Switzerland, and I had the chance to talk to Doc. It turned out he'd started the book in the '60s with Marty Cantine, who lived in Bankok. Unfortunately Marty died some years ago, but his papers, and the taped recollections Doc had sent him, survived and have been incorporated into this text.

Later that year, Doc and I agreed to try and continue the book, despite living on opposite sides of the Atlantic. Since then, we have kept up a regular correspondence, and the present book is the result. I'm grateful to Derek Drescher and BBC Radio 3 for help in recording further interviews with Doc, broadcast in 1993 as a three-part series *Swing That Music*, and subsequently incorporated into the text.

I'm also grateful to the many people who have helped along the way, but especially Georgina Marson of Oxford Brookes University and Stephen McGinty of Nottingham University, (who both helped transcribe taped interviews,) Chuck and Jane Folds, Nancy Miller Elliott, and Howard Rye, for his careful reading of the text as well as the discography. He and I are grateful to the staff of the Guildhall Library, City of London (Lloyd's Marine Collection) for confirming the voyage of the *Schodack*, a Philadelphia registered 3116 tonner, from Le Havre on 9 September 1939, to New York, arriving 21 September. In various printed accounts, there has been some confusion about the dates of Doc's trip to Europe before World War Two, and the time he joined Teddy Wilson. This shows (as Doc has always maintained) that he was indeed in France after the outbreak of war, which was declared on 3 September.

Above all, I'm grateful to Doc Cheatham for his endless

patience and kindness, while this was being written.

The pictures are all from Doc Cheatham's personal collection and are reproduced by permission. We are grateful to Nancy Miller Elliott for the use of her photographs. We have made efforts to ensure all copyright owners have given permission, but if any have inadvertently been overlooked we will be happy to include the appropriate acknowledgement in every future printing.

Alyn Shipton
Oxford, 1995

Postscript

Doc Cheatham died on 2 June 1997, aged 91, after collapsing shortly after playing at Washington's Blues Alley club the night before. Following on almost directly from a week's engagement at the Iridium in New York, he was touring with Nicholas Payton's quartet, to promote the album they had recently made together (one of a very small number of recent sessions not included in the recording chronology at the end of the book). I spoke to Doc during the New York residency, and he was his usual optimistic self, looking forward to future plans for playing and travelling. In that conversation, as in almost every one I had with him, he expressed his delight that his memoirs had seen their way into print during his lifetime.

At the request of Doc's daughter, Alicia, we have included Chuck Folds' tribute as an introduction to this paperback edition. It was first published in the July edition of Gene Lees' *Jazzletter* and is reprinted by permission. It includes details of the memorial fund established in Doc's memory to sponsor young musicians. Many of Doc's friends contributed at the start of the fund and it was able to begin almost immediately, by sponsoring two students to attend the summer 1997 jazz workshop in Litchfield.

A.S.

Introduction To The Paperback Edition

by Chuck Folds
pianist in Doc Cheatham's New York Quartet

When Doc Cheatham died, my wife Jane and I lost the best friend we've ever had. We met him five months before we met each other, in 1972, and at our twenty–third wedding anniversary dinner last night, we kept seeing the sadness behind our smiles.

Except for Jane and my parents and brother, I've never had a longer, closer association with anyone than with Doc. From the time we started playing regularly together in 1975 to my last gig with him, on May 25 at Sweet Basil, it was rare that two weeks would pass without our doing at least one gig together.

Virtually everything I called remarkable about Doc when he was 82 (in a July 1987 piece about him for Gene Lees' *Jazzletter*) still held when he was almost 92. His only progressive physical problem was arthritis, chiefly in his knees. Just listen to anything he plays on his last record, the Verve CD *Doc Cheatham and Nicholas Payton*, and tell me that anyone in his nineties could possibly play the trumpet with that much vigor and grace. He defied all odds, and we will *never* see the likes of him again.

There was so much to him. I've never known a person with a finer sense of humanity. No matter how much he was praised, he always regarded himself as no better than the next guy. I've never known anyone more honest with both himself and his fellow man, and I mean unswerving 100–percent honesty. There was not a *hint* of anything devious about him. His ethics were not situational; he cast no aspersions.

Doc looked at life straight on, with eyes open. He had no illusions, and no bad habits for a wounded psyche to escape to. He was always open to suggestion (perhaps one of the secrets to his longevity) and he faced difficulties with a strong and buoyant spirit.

Doc's daughter, Alicia, is setting up a music scholarship fund in his name. (Adolphus Anthony "Doc" Cheatham Scholarship Memorial Fund, c/o Huntingdon National Bank, PO Box 490047,

Leesburg, Florida, 34749, USA.

St. Peter's Church on Lexington Avenue, the musicians' church, is dedicating this year's *All Night Soul* to Doc.

James Browne, Sweet Basil's co–manager, has announced that the Sunday jazz brunch Doc started there nearly 17 years ago will continue, in his honor and spirit, with his rhythm section (me on piano, Earl May on bass, and Jackie Williams on drums) and a guest horn player, under the brand name Chuck Folds and Friends. For the first several Sundays these guest players will be, more or less alternating, trumpeters Irvin Stokes and Spanky Davis and trombonist Benny Powell. There will be others. These guys were Doc's favorites and most frequent subs.

From my long experience of playing with dozens of Doc's contemporaries, I'm convinced that the incredible influence of Louis Armstrong on those guys, especially trumpeters, was at least as strong, if not stronger, than the influence of any later dominant figure: Prez, Bird, Miles, whoever. And we should remember that after Doc's generation there were several models to choose from. In Doc's time there was only one. There was Bix, too, a brilliant shining star, but not of Louis' magnitude. Isn't it interesting that, though inescapably influenced by one man, Louis, every fine swing era trumpeter found his own immediately recognizable identity? Red Allen sounded like no one but Red Allen; the same for Buck Clayton and Rex Stewart and Shorty Baker. And today, with all the choices and accessible information about this music, I think the main message got lost. Somebody who can pull the right strings should get a search party together and go looking for it and tell the kids about it, before it's too late. Which, by now, it might be. But hope springs eternal.

At his memorial service at St. Peter's, I made these observations:

Doc was the best listener I've ever known. And that quiet charm of his. How does such a gentle, unassuming, serene man light up a room when he walks into it? He did, every time. Maybe it was that serenity, reaching out like a subtle magnet.

Whenever I was with Doc, be it on a gig or in an airport, I felt that somehow everything had a kind of sparkle to it. The day was special because he was there. I agree with William, his

viii

son–in–law, who says that no matter what was happening, Doc always seemed to have a certain understanding of everything that was going on.

There was something very spiritual about Doc. I often had the feeling that someone from up above was watching over him for us . . .

I revered Doc, and I loved him , and I just plain liked him.

He loved life, and he prevailed.

As sad as Doc's death has left me, in whatever trail of thoughts I follow, I always end up seeing him with that characteristic sparkle in his eye and that gentle smile. Nearly a quarter of a century of lucky memories.

July 1997

1
Nashville Days

My mother's name was Alice Anthony Cheatham. She was part Indian, mixed with oriental, and she taught school in her home town of Atlanta, Georgia. My father, Marshall Ney Cheatham, was born in Tennessee. Our ancestors go back to Cheatham County, located in the hills, which is rich in past Indian cultures. He played mandolin and was a barber on the riverboats. He had a shop in Nashville for years, serving whites only, with a partner named Bibb: Cheatham and Bibb's Barber Shop.

His hours at the shop were from seven in the morning until seven at night, and he stayed open until midnight on Saturdays. He would always pull down the shades on time every night so no one could see in the shop, and finish off the customers that were inside. Sometimes he'd wait for special customers who were late. There were four chairs, and two bath tubs on the second floor for those who wanted to clean up, as many of his customers were farmers. As a teenager I would shine shoes in the shop on Saturdays, and at times scrubbed the customers' backs when requested - the tips were good. There was a tailor shop on the third floor.

Pa would go straight home at night, tired out, but he managed to keep the yard clean and the grass cut. He was a good father, but a quiet man, who seldom had much to say. His life was a hard one. He was not a drinking man, but he kept a nip at the house for emergencies. He was a great wine maker, using his cellar for his makings. He was not a church-going man either, but most Sundays he would take his grip of barber tools and cut the hair of the sick. And after he'd shaved them or cut their hair, he wouldn't charge them anything. If they wanted to give him a dollar or two, he'd take it. But he had a lot of friends. He was a real diplomat, and he taught me a lot of the things that I guess I feel I've inherited from him. I don't hate anyone, I don't dislike anyone, and that has helped me. My father was very well-liked and got everything he wanted from the whites. Even our house, which was in a white neighborhood, was bought by his white friends and sold to Pa.

But I'll go back to the time I was born, June 13th, 1905. I was born on the Murfreesboro Pike, in a neighborhood in the country. The people round there were mostly white farmers. There were very few negroes round that vicinity. I was quite young when we lived there, because when I was still a small boy my father moved into Nashville, on University Street. The neighborhood was mixed. It was white and colored, but it wasn't well-to-do white people, because they lived out in what they then called Bellmead, and that was all exclusively white out there. Most of Nashville, (East Nashville, South Nashville, West Nashville), was mixed. We had a white family living across the street from us, one even living next door. And all us kids, we played together. We didn't know anything about white or black, we were too young.

I've got to say Nashville was a heck of a fine city. Of course they had segregation laws which everyone had to abide by, but we were allowed to go anywhere we wanted other than some of the theaters and restaurants. There was one area of downtown that was more or less entirely black, on the edge of the main downtown area. The streetcar transfer station was nearby, and on 4th Avenue and Cedar Street all the black folks would hang out, eating ice-cream, drinking sodas, and looking sharp. There were black barbers, dentists, lawyers, beauty parlors there, and it was a busy area. Saturdays were the days when it was best to hang out there, with the streets alive until late in the night. At midnight the area was cleared of all blacks, and the white cops would occasionally run in any blacks who were caught out after that time.

There was a big YMCA building in that part of town, which had about six floors, but it was poorly run, and it was not too safe to be going up in that building. On the ground floor of that building was the People's Savings Bank, the only black bank in Nashville, although very few black people actually used it, preferring to put their money in white banks. Above that area, everything was white. Everyone was allowed in the department stores, but if you were black, you couldn't go in there and try

2

anything on. If you wanted a hat, shoes, gloves, clothes, you had to pay for it, and if it didn't fit, well, that was too bad.

We could go in any restaurant, in the front, and order some food and take it out. We couldn't sit down. And we couldn't sit in the front of the white theater. We had to go out in the alley and walk round to what we called the "Buzzard's Roost". It took up to fifteen minutes to get up there. The whites could come to our theater when they wanted, and to our dances when big names came there. But these were the laws of the land, so naturally everybody abided by them.

My brother's name was Marshall Ney Cheatham Jr. He was two years older than I, and eventually he became a dental surgeon. He took after father, and was stern and dignified. To finance himself through college he worked as a Pullman porter, and later at the Dupont powder plant. He practised in Chicago and St. Louis. He never got around the world much, just stuck to dentistry. But he was a great man for mechanical and electrical things. He could take an automobile motor to pieces and put it back together. I don't think he ever had any training in that kind of thing, it was just natural. He built a boat and did a lot of fishing when he retired back to Nashville. But four years after he retired he died. Music was never his thing, but we were very close. I could never think of retiring to Nashville myself, because I inherited a touch of asthma from my mother, but I'm only really badly affected in Nashville. I think about my brother, sometimes, and say to myself: "What the hell, I'm glad I didn't go to medical school." Because, well, look at the way medicine is now. I think a black doctor has a hard time even training today. Taking medical or dental courses has gotten very expensive for black students today.

I don't know of too many relatives that I have still living, but there are a few Cheathams around. I have two cousins in St. Louis, who were the daughters of my father's brother, Dr. Anderson Cheatham. A few years ago I met a whole family of Cheathams that came to Sweet Basil, where I play in New York, and they were Indians. All of them were wearing Indian dress, and they came from that same area as my family, upstate in

3

Virginia and Tennessee. They wanted to know all about my family history, but I really don't know anything about my Indian ancestry, except my grandfather on my father's side was an Indian, but he actually came from Oklahoma. Another time, I met Jimmy and Jeannie Cheatham out in San Diego, they're musicians, and they hail from the same part of the country as well. I guess back in those far off days there was a lot of hanky-panky going on, integration between the Indians, the black folks, the white folks. I wish there was a book written on that area where the Cheathams come from that would tell the story straight.

My mother's family, the Anthonys, were from Atlanta. There were offshoots of her family called Scotts and Derricots. The son of my first cousin on my mother's side, George Derricot, was very talented as a musician and entertainer. He played the comb and tissue paper, and made it sound like a trumpet and all sorts of other instruments. He danced and sang, and he had a saxophone which he wore out. He is the only relative I have that was musically inclined apart from my father playing mandolin on the boats, but I never heard him to tell how good he was. The only problem with George was that he was afraid to venture far from Atlanta, so he never got to Chicago or New York. I don't think he read music particularly well, but he had great natural talent. He was a hustler, buying and selling things, and he had a hot dog stall out by the military base there. In the end he retired to Honolulu. I didn't see him again before he died a few years ago, but we corresponded.

So I was the only musician in our immediate family. Many of the rest of my relatives distinguished themselves in other fields. My mother's cousin, for example, Martha Brown, was a university librarian at A. and I. State College in Nashville. Now there's a library built on the campus there dedicated to her. My adopted sister, Helda Little, had a nurses' home named for her at the George W. Hubbard Hospital on the Meharry campus. Her name is up on top of it. My family never thought too much of music. Over the years things changed, but I don't think they thought I belonged in their society in Nashville because I was a jazz player and I was like the devil.

4

When I was growing up, we had segregated schools, naturally; so did the rest of the South, but the black and white students got along fine, got along beautifully together. They still do so. We had just about the same kind of education they had. We didn't have a lot of new books. Most of our books were hand-downs, in good condition, from the white schools. Our teachers were excellent. Our principals were excellent. And of course we didn't know any different. If you're born and raised in a town like that, you accept it as part of your life, like it's supposed to be.

Of course if you had the opportunity to go North then you could see the difference and it'd kind of upset you a little bit. It'd be hard for you to understand why, unless you got right down to it and read the laws of the land in the South. But Nashville was an exceptionally fine city and I guess the schools there had a lot to do with it. There were schools all over the place. They had Meharry Medical College - that was a black school - and they had Hubbard Hospital. Many fine nurses came out of Hubbard Hospital. We had Waldrom University campus, we had Fisk University, we had A. and I. State. Then we had high schools, all the grade schools, grammar schools. Those were all black schools. But I remember when I was a kid there were white students at Meharry Medical College. I recall that. We lived practically on the campus of Meharry Medical College. But the black students couldn't go to the white schools, of course. Not at that time. Now, of course, that's changed.

All the trolley cars had a sign on the front that said "White", and a sign in the back that said "Black". Whoever were the majority of people had preference on the trolley cars. Sometimes in some areas you'd have whites standing up and negroes occupying the whole car. There was some robbing, but I don't remember a lynching, race riots, or anything unnatural when I was a kid.

At the age of fourteen I took up the cornet through the B.F.S. Club (the "Bright Future Stars") which was organised by Mr. Meredith, Dean at the Phillips Chapel at Nashville, for the neighborhood kids. He formed it to compete with another such band in Franklin, Tennessee. It brought us all together, and we

5

had instruments given or donated to us. Some of them were very good, we certainly had lots of them. I selected the drums when each kid initially took what he wanted to play, but Mr. N. C. Davis, who came in as our teacher, took the drums away and gave me a cornet.

I was playing it in a week's time by ear. The first song I played was called "Action Quick Step". We had practice once a week and we had to pay 25 cents for each practice. Mr. Davis didn't go into all the details of reading. I don't know why, because he was a professional trumpet player. He just figured that we'd catch on, without a whole lot of explanation, which is what a lot of kids did. I was one of the worst readers. I didn't even try to read. I was so elated over playing notes on the horn, playing it without music, I didn't even think it was necessary to read.

So we had a nice little juvenile band there. We played a lot of elementary military music and finally the band started sounding pretty good. We had uniforms and we played for the county fairs on the days that negroes could attend. We'd sit around in circles and play little light classical things and marches. Sometimes we'd play in the city on holidays: we'd all get around one of the street corners and play, and the whites would throw pennies and nickels, dimes and dollars. They respected us. They enjoyed us. And they thought it was a great thing for the community.

We got to the stage, as kids, where we were all jazz crazy. Our Mr. Meredith objected to that because in those days jazz was called "sin music". So he forbade us to play jazz and that's finally what broke up the juvenile band.

I think I and maybe two or three others out of that whole group continued. Immediately I got a saxophone - my Dad bought a soprano saxophone for me - and I started playing it without even knowing what note I was making or anything. It seemed to fall right in with the trumpet and I worked out how the lower register of the saxophone corresponded with the notes I could make using the three valves of the trumpet. So I played both those instruments pretty nice for that time, and when the juvenile band broke up, I started playing with older men. There were quite a few musicians who played in circuses, and during the off season they'd come to Nashville and rest, and we'd play together in the park, or parades, or little things like that.

Sometimes the Ringling Brothers would come through Nashville and they would hire us on one of their circus wagons during the parade. People would always call on this band. I was the smallest. I was a kid, but I was playing with this band for a long time. A lot of the men were heavy drinkers. I observed how they felt, and how they played when they were like that, and so I made up my mind then: "I'm not going to be like that. I want to be a good musician, so I'll leave the whisky alone." And I have done.

I got to a stage where I wanted to play more jazz. So I started to play a few dances around Nashville with Mr. Braxton Murrell. He was my math teacher at Pearl High in Nashville and he played piano. We played for the rich and the poor, the nice and the rough, and it got rough as hell at times. We sometimes had to play overtime, with no pay, at the threat of being shot. Mr. Murrell had a lot of contacts in Nashville with the white people. He'd play the Elks club and he built up quite a name for himself round there, mainly on Fridays and Saturdays. He would always take me and we'd make maybe two or three dollars a night. I did that for a long time.

Around the same time, I made a radio. I saved all of my money and bought all the components to make a crystal set. I think Paul Whiteman was the first band I heard on the radio and he had a trumpet player called Louis Panico. I got a real kick out of Panico's playing and I started looking for Whiteman's recordings, especially if Panico was on them. Then I heard Johnny Dunn. He had a recording of "Bugle Blues" that was sensational. I bought his records and learnt to play all of his stuff. My reading was still poor, but I had a good ear.

Nashville was a pretty dead town when the schools were closed during the summer months. Then when Meharry opened and the freshmen came to Nashville, there was plenty going on. There were some very fine musicians at Meharry, like Bill Tyson, a violinist who was a fine doctor, and his brother, who played drums, or Charles Whitby, an excellent pianist. Then there was

Jimmy Strong on tenor saxophone, who later did a lot of recording with Louis Armstrong in Chicago. He was a fine saxophone player, but he was studying dentistry. We had Herbert Bloom from New Orleans, who was one of the great pianists, D.M.E. Smith from Illinois on guitar and banjo, and Bill Woods (who studied pharmacy) was also a fine pianist, and, like Jimmy Strong, later played with Bessie Smith. There weren't any bass players or drummers among the Meharry students, but we had good drummers in Nashville, including Hosea Duff and O.B. Davis.

There weren't so many cornet players either, but they learned I was nearby, so they had me up there to join the school band, which played every first Sunday, just before the president, George W. Hubbard, gave his address. A lot of the musicians there didn't know if I was going to the school or not, because there were so many students there. But a funny thing about those students, they called one another "Doctor" as soon as they met. So I became "Doc" Cheatham and there was Doc Tyson, Doc Woods and Doc Bloom. They didn't worry about your first name - just everybody was called "Doc". So that's where I got that from, and soon my mother called me that, my father, all of them, in a nice way.

My parents encouraged me to enter Meharry and study as a pharmacist, which I had in mind. But my heart wasn't in it after I'd started in music. I played with the school band every first Sunday up there, doing light overtures, things like that. I couldn't read a note, and I don't really know how I did it, but I played all those parts. Then I met some musicians from Fisk University. (The great saxophonist Willie Smith was at Fisk at that time.) Sometimes we'd play for their proms, holiday things, school things. We'd sometimes get together a twelve piece band to play for their dances. It was very nice.

I also worked with a honky-tonk piano player named Dan Stafford, who was a barber at the YMCA. He had a bald head, only one leg, and looked like Jack Johnson. He had a lot of jive talk about how great he was, but he couldn't read a note. He played pretty good piano, though, mostly blues-type things, and he would get a lot of jobs because the white people liked him. He was a honky-tonk kind of guy, but he got a lot of wonderful jobs around Nashville in country clubs and private homes, and he took me along with him. Dan and I had things pretty well sewed up in Nashville. He had a brother, Louis Stafford, who played tenor saxophone. He reminded me so much of many of the rock and roll saxophonists of today. He couldn't read a note either, but his playing had plenty of drive and swing to it. So, in Nashville I did pretty good.

One summer I worked in Louisville, Kentucky, with Ferman Tapp. I played coal-mine district dances in Kentucky very often. One night we could find no place to sleep. In order for us to get in out of the cold, the sheriff charged us with shooting dice and locked us up. The next morning the judge released us. For a while I had a job outside music, working at a creosote plant, but then I got a job at the Eight Mile House with Dicky Wells.

But I wasn't satisfied, because I didn't find myself getting where I wanted to get. So I took my soprano saxophone and put it in a case, and I got a tenor saxophone - or rather a C-melody. I went down to the Bijou Theater and started playing in the theater, in the pit band.

The Bijou Theater was on the TOBA circuit. It was downtown, below Cedar Street. That was an all-black street of bars and run down shops. No decent black person would go on Cedar Street. They had a three-piece band in the theater there: drums, piano, and a cornet player. The pianist, Maggie Hargraves, knew how to play for the shows and acts, and she played heck out of that piano. There was a fine cornet player. His name was George Jefferson, and he looked like a creole. I think he came from Louisiana. He wasn't a jazz player, but he could really blow. So I went in there on tenor saxophone. I wasn't getting paid, but I wanted the experience and so I played for all the shows. Sometimes the shows would bring big bands, and we'd augment the bands on stage or in the pit. I had a heck of a time playing shows. All the blues singers came through: Bessie Smith, Clara Smith, Ethel Waters, Ida Cox - all of them - and Joe Smith with his cornet. He really thrilled me with his plunger playing. So I got a plunger and started doing the same thing with my trumpet.

9

I still could not read and I was not interested in learning to read at that time. During school vacation in 1924 I went to Atlantic City. I hadn't ever really been much out of Nashville, so this was one of the first places I visited for any length of time. I'd never seen any place like Atlantic City before. I'd never seen the ocean before in my life. So it was all very new to me and very exciting. I had three or four weeks to stay there before I had to go back to school. I was pushing chairs on the Boardwalk for 50 cents an hour and hopping bells at a small hotel to earn my keep. But I took both of my horns with me and I played a few gigs with a little local band there. I don't know exactly who was responsible, but someone told me that the bandleader Charlie Johnson was in town, and he needed a saxophone player. I could play the C-melody pretty well by that time, so I was hired to play saxophone at the Paradise Club with Charlie Johnson's Orchestra. I played the first set which was for dancing, and it went well. They liked me a lot until they put the show music in front of me. I couldn't read a note of it, and he fired me right away. Charlie never hired me again. In his later years he became a beggar and a drunk and I remember giving him money at times.

I began to see I wanted to do better than this and learn to read. I got busy, with help, and found it lots of fun. I learned from a girl piano player I was gigging with up there in Atlantic City. She taught me, and I caught on very easily. She was a nice pianist, playing good piano.

Then I went to St. Louis with John "Bearcat" Williams and his Synco Jazzers. This was during the summertime on a little TOBA show. The TOBA was a circuit that kept all of its shows and acts working but also kept them broke. Nobody much was getting paid anything, just a few dollars now and then. Although I was able to read by this time, in fact we didn't have to read on that show. Everything was faking. Mary Lou Williams was in the show, she was the pianist. We had to play in the pit. We didn't play on the stage, but even so they blacked all our faces. Even John Williams's face, they put black paint on top of that. He was so black nobody could see him. We had to do an overture, jumping up and down in the pit, playing some tune. When we got to St. Louis, my father's brother, Dr. Anderson Cheatham, heard I was there. He pulled me right out of the pit, put me on a train and sent me back to Nashville. He didn't want that low type of career for me. He said he wanted me to be a pharmacist. I obeyed him and went back to Nashville, but I went right back into the theater when I got there!

I was there about two or three months, and then a show came through: Sunshine Sammy, a dancer and a comedian who was one of the famous "Our Gang" comedy kids. He was the only black member of that group in those days. He was actually a great dancer and very funny. His father used to organize the shows on the TOBA circuit, and he figured they could make a lot of money on the tour because he was well-known and well-liked. With his films and everything he should have been a hit with a revue on the TOBA. He had this little show with Glenn Cheesman and Harold Barkay singing, and a few chorus girls, but of course Sammy was the main attraction. It was a good little show.

Marion Hardy had the band with the show. The featured singer was Monette Moore. He had a trumpet player, himself, and Charlie Turner on the bass. (He was the same Charlie Turner that later worked with Fats Waller, and he opened a restaurant up in Harlem that was featured in that song "At the Fat Man's".) Marion liked my tenor saxophone playing and asked me to go on the road with them. Well, I had to get permission from my father, this time. I went down to the barber shop, and finally he said I could go. He really wanted me to go to college, but he agreed when he realized it was hopeless to stop me. It was my first job as a professional musician, playing sax. Well, again we weren't really getting paid. We got accommodation and ten dollars, something like that; we weren't receiving a salary. But as long as I could eat, sleep and play, that's all I cared about. When we got to Chicago, we decided to disband, so they broke up the show and everybody went their own way, but I had made it to Chicago and I decided to stay there.

2
Chicago

When the show broke up, the only one of us to land a job was the pianist, Jerome Carrington. He was an excellent player, and he immediately got hired by Charlie Cook. Doc Cook's Dreamland Orchestra was one of the big-time bands there in Chicago.

The rest of us in Marion Hardy's group decided to stick together, and Jerome found us a house where we could stay and where we didn't have to worry about paying the rent until we started to work. We only had sandwiches and things to live on, but every now and then, perhaps every couple of weeks, one of us would get a job. We'd bring the money back and split it and buy beans and things. There was a little restaurant in Chicago called Poor Me, and for 50 cents one of us would go up there and bring back enough food for the rest of us to eat.

When I got to Chicago, I only had one suit. Pretty soon after we arrived I went out and got a job washing dishes, to try and make some money. The restaurant was down in the Loop, and I got there by about six o'clock in the morning to start work. I sat out in the back where all the washing up was done and nothing happened. Then, around noon, the rush came in. I washed, I washed, and I washed. I never saw so many dishes. They didn't have machines back in those days, so I was washing everything by hand. I got grease and water and mess all over my clothes. So I went to the owner and I said "I can't go home like this, I need something to wear, because these clothes are all that I have."

He gave me three dollars, and I left and never went back. I bought some cheap jeans, which were about a dollar then, but I vowed I'd never go back to washing dishes again.

There were four or five of us staying together in the house. We went along like that for a long time, and I couldn't get any work playing music in Chicago. That didn't really matter to me, because I was so excited listening to the greatest musicians I'd ever heard. There were people like Freddie Keppard, Louis Armstrong, Jimmie Noone. I got so excited listening to them I didn't do too much except sleeping and eating. But I didn't eat enough and I grew very thin, and at one point I barely had the strength to stand up.

I thought I ought to join the Musicians' Union, so I could get a job. The president was a woman, named Lottie Hightower, and she said, "You can't work in Chicago, because you're not from New Orleans."

Al Capone had opened all these clubs and sent for the best of the New Orleans musicians to come and play there. Almost all of the musicians seemed to be from New Orleans at the time.

So Miss Hightower says, "Anyway, where are you from?"

And I told her, Nashville, Tennessee.

"Well," she said, "I graduated myself from Fisk University!" And she gave me a card because of that. It was a temporary card, but it allowed me to work and she took care of the price. She was a piano player, and once in a while I played with her.

Then she introduced me to Lil Armstrong. Lil was also a graduate of Fisk and she was a fine person. She knew I wasn't doing too well in Chicago, and she threw as many gigs my way as she could. Even then, I wasn't making much, I wouldn't make $20, except now and then.

Finally I got a job playing saxophone with Albert Wynn's band which was working at the Dreamland. At first they refused me, but Louis Armstrong himself sent word and said "Let him work!" Because Louis was a great friend of Al Capone's, when he asked for something he wanted, it would usually happen. So he told me I could go and work at the Dreamland.

Albert Wynn already had a cornetist, so with him I stuck to playing saxophone. The musicians in the band were very friendly and relaxed towards one another. As I got known in Chicago, I found virtually all the musicians I met to be equally friendly, which was a big contrast to what I found a few years later in New York. There were so many cliques there that if you didn't belong to the right one nobody would hire you. They wouldn't have cared if you could play like Gabriel, if you weren't in the clique they wouldn't hire you. I remember being in clubs in Harlem where people from downtown called to get groups for certain engagements. They'd keep those to themselves, wouldn't let you in on them to save their lives.

In Chicago, Albert Wynn's band was quite different. In fact it was a nice little band, with Jimmy McKendrick on piano, Silas White on bass, Don Brown on saxophone, Al himself on trombone and Ben Thigpen on drums. We got along pretty well at the Dreamland, but we weren't really getting paid there either. The owner of the club would give us a few dollars, and put this on his books. But he had the books arranged so that after we'd signed them he would enter any amount he wanted up above the signature. We didn't know this, and we weren't making much although we were at the Dreamland for a little while.

While I was with Albert Wynn's band, we made a recording with Ma Rainey. I played soprano saxophone, and from somewhere we got a musical saw player. With the vibrato from that musical saw, and my vibrato on the soprano, it made the thing sound terrible. I've never heard anything so bad in all my life, but I listen to it just for fun once in a while, because it's my only record on the saxophone.

There were lots of little back alleys in Chicago, that ran behind some of the clubs where great musicians were playing. I sometimes slept outside the Sunset, where Louis worked. His playing upset me so much I decided to give up the saxophone, and concentrate on the trumpet, so I sold my C-melody to Thornton Blue, who was a great clarinet and saxophone player in those days. I think Barney Bigard was actually the greatest tenor man I heard at that time. I wish there were more recordings of what he could do on the tenor.

I heard Freddie Keppard on trumpet. He was amazing. One night word got around he'd blown a note so loud that he blew his mute right out of the end of his horn and it sailed away across the floor of the nightclub he was playing at. Everybody in town ran to hear Freddie Keppard that night. Next day all you could hear was people talking about Freddie and his mute. The place was packed for some time afterwards but he never did do it again.

I also heard King Oliver. Even today I have a mute that used to belong to Joe Oliver. I'd hear him at the Royal Gardens, but although I'd go along there to see him, we never were introduced. I was such a fan of his, I used to follow him down the street after work. I knew his valet, and it was he who gave me the mute. I wanted to hear what Oliver was into, musically, but I was reluctant to disturb him after he'd played a job. Later the Sunset was his second home, there in Chicago.

I used to hear all the guys play. It was easy to go upstairs at the Apex Club and hear Jimmie Noone. Jimmie was very nice to me and I could sit around and listen for a while, unless the club needed my seat. At the other clubs, it was more difficult. I didn't have any money, but a guy told me how to act when you were broke. He told me to walk right in like I owned the place and nobody would bother me. I'd walk in with my arms folded and act like I had a pocketful of money. I got away with it until they all caught on to me, and then it was back to the alleys behind the clubs. I occasionally worked with Jimmie, and with trombonist Gerald Reeves, Tiny Parham, and Gerald's brother, Reuben Reeves.

It was Louis who was the talk of the town. He was playing with Carroll Dickerson, and there were two piano players - Earl Hines and Willy Hamby. That was some band, and my buddy Shirley Clay played with them. He sat beside Louis in the trumpet section, which was what all trumpeters wanted to do. Guys would play for no pay if they could sit alongside Louis. Quite a few of the players who did this began to develop some of Louis' habits - I mean things he used to do that nobody else did. I would have given anything for the opportunity to sit with Louis. We all play some of Louis at one time or another. We have to, because he was the greatest trumpet player in all the world.

As well as working at the Sunset, Louis was featured with Erskine Tate's Orchestra at the Vendome Theater. In fact he was featured there for quite a long time. I guess he and Albert Wynn were pals, because one day Louis came by the Dreamland and asked me if I'd sub for him at the Vendome. I got there about half an hour before show time, and Erskine's brother Jimmy, who played trumpet with the band asked me what I was doing. When I told him, Jimmy showed me the charts they were using, as they played for the movies that were showing as well as doing band specialties.

The show began, and there was standing room only. About that time, Louis was being featured on a tune called "Poor Little Rich Girl", which I knew well, because I'd spent everything I had going to the Vendome myself to hear him. Well, we got to the point in the show when it was time for Louis's feature. The lights in the pit went up, and the band went into "Poor Little Rich Girl". The people were screaming and hollering for Louis, and as I stood up they screamed "Louis! Louis!"

When they got a good look at me, the screaming died right away to nothing. Then and there, I wished there was a hole in the floor and I was small enough to fit through it. But although I wasn't yet a good jazz player, I knew my horn, and I played fine, playing Louis's part. I played it like I played it, because nobody in the world could play like Louis. I guess Erskine must have been satisfied, because I subbed for Louis again a couple of times after that.

The band at the Vendome didn't receive me very well. I didn't care, because I knew I was going to get something to eat, and I hadn't been eating anything. I got $85 for that job. But I was curious why he had sent for me, and why the band seemed hostile.

I said to myself, "With all those guys round here, like George Mitchell, Natty Dominique, all hanging round, why did he choose me?"

I didn't learn until years later when I was working with Johnny Guarnieri on a concert. He was a very great friend of Louis, and he told me what Louis had told him. Apparently Louis felt the other New Orleans musicians didn't treat him right. So it was an unwritten law, he didn't hire them, so he hired me instead. It didn't really matter to Louis who I was, he didn't care much what I did, he just hired me.

Anyhow, I thought it was very nice to be given that chance. I never had the opportunity, after Johnny talked to me, to thank Louis, because when I started thinking about it, Louis was already in the hospital and he died before I could get to see him.

None of the other trumpeters in Chicago then had the soul

16

that Louis had in his playing. Not even Keppard and Oliver. Perhaps it was jealousy over Louis's success that meant the other New Orleans players didn't treat him right. But of course, at the time I didn't know about that. I was just listening and learning. I wanted to know all about the New Orleans tunes and I kept a notebook while I played with Al Wynn to jot down many of the old New Orleans pieces they played.

I don't know what it is, but there's a difference between black musicians and white musicians. I can tell a black musician from a white musician blindfolded, any time. There's always a little bitty something that'll come out from white musicians, especially trumpet players, however great they are and however good they are. I met Bunny Berigan and Bix Beiderbecke, and although I didn't meet them face to face until later, I was also in many of the same places at the same time as the young Benny Goodman and Frankie Trumbauer.

They were all star musicians, but with Louis on the scene, everyone was listening to him because he had so much to offer. To me, Bunny Berigan was a great trumpet player. There was something about him that reminded me of a black player but I could hear the difference. With Bix you could hear the difference straight away. In fact we had some black players that played very much like Bix, but they were never recognized. Nobody knew anything about Cuban Bennett, he was a cousin to Benny Carter, but he could play all those beautiful chord changes we associate with Bix. Bobby Hackett was a great player. Terrific. But there was a difference. I can always tell. I guess that's nature, because blacks and whites never did think alike anyway. They just can't. Too many generations separate us.

What really counts, though, is the difference in feeling that comes out of the bell of a horn. You can always feel that. And I'm not just talking about trumpeters. Take clarinets, for instance. I'm not thinking so much of the old style of New Orleans clarinet, but the very technical styles that came in after Benny Goodman and Artie Shaw and Jimmy Dorsey. They've got the better of the black musician, by and large, as far as the technique's concerned although we had a few great technicians that took the instrument in a different direction. Buster Bailey, for example, or Ed Inge. But I think my favourite clarinet player of all time was Benny Carter. I don't know of anyone who could play more clarinet than Benny, and now he's taken the trumpet and the alto saxophone and he's running everybody crazy with them.

3
Philadelphia, Europe and Sam Wooding

Things got pretty bad in Chicago, I was losing a lot of weight because I wasn't eating anything much. But I got so thin and sickly I guess God looked down on me, and someone sent me a ticket to Philadelphia. A young woman out of St. Paul, Minnesota, had come to Chicago looking for a trumpet player to work with a band. I don't know how in the world she did this, but she ran into the right person that knew me. He said, "Doc Cheatham's here, he's a trumpet player." So she came at me and she says, "We have a job for you in Philadelphia, I have your ticket and everything."

It was to play with a guy by the name of Bobby Lee, who had a band there called Bobby Lee's Cotton Pickers. He had a job at Sea Girt, New Jersey, at the Sea Girt Inn, every summer. So I went to Philadelphia, where Bobby was playing at the Cinderella Inn and rehearsed for the job in New Jersey. There was a big floor show, with plenty of pretty chicks in the chorus, and I was reading well by then and everybody liked my playing. At the end of the week at the Cinderella, there wasn't any money. The club was closed by the law, and I was still broke. That band was Juan Tizol, Lincoln Mills, Joe Hayman, a boy named Stafford from Philadelphia on bass, Harry Marsh on drums. A fellow named Fernando Arbello was on that job, too, and Jerry Blake. I got him in on things, because our friendship worked like that. We all moved to New Jersey and played there one season. When I arrived, I had no money at all, and so I stayed with Bobby Lee at his house. I didn't even think about money in those days. I worked with Bobby until the place closed, then after that was over the band broke up.

That must have been in the latter part of 1926, because then I ran into Wilbur De Paris. He was working at the Pearl Theater in Philadelphia, and he immediately hired me. He was looking for a trumpet player to play alongside Sidney, his brother. He never had too much faith in Sidney. Sidney wasn't very punctual. He used to show if he wanted to, and if he didn't feel like it, he didn't turn up. That sort of disturbed Wilbur. So I played in his band, which was called the Cotton Pickers also. We worked at the Pearl Theater and did little parades around Philadelphia.

Sidney was a great trumpet player. I never heard anyone else quite like him in all my life. He had a style that nobody, but nobody, played. It was a great style, and he is certainly missed. I felt very much at home playing alongside him, because he seemed to speak the language I understood. Sidney and I played very well together, and Wilbur gave me more opportunities to play solos than anyone I had worked with.

As well as Sidney, there was another trumpeter in Wilbur's band in Philadelphia. A very gentlemanly, well-trained musician, who was also an athlete. His name was Bill Dillard, and perhaps he had more sense than the rest of us because he studied to be an actor. He had the natural talent for it. Later, he worked with Don Redman and Teddy Hill, a lot of the popular bands around New York. As a young man, he was a weightlifter, and he looked like Charles Atlas! He played his butt off on the trumpet, and then all of a sudden he went off and started to study theatrics. He got onto the Broadway stage, acting, sometimes singing (he had a beautiful baritone voice), and sometimes even playing his horn. I thought he was a simply marvellous trumpet player and he's less well-known than he should be. Now he's an old-timer like me, and he's often off round the world touring. He played for some years in that show "One Mo' Time" in New York and in Europe. I think his name should be brought up more.

Although I had a job with Wilbur, I was still very poor, and very thin. I did one gig in Indianapolis and I had so little money I went fishing in a little creek for crawdads. That's the way I ate then. I lost so much weight you'd be surprised. So with Wilbur I stayed at his house.

Wilbur's wife was a really wonderful looking girl. She cooked for me all the time. I ate breakfast with them, and dinner and everything. Now all the time I was staying there, Wilbur had this filing cabinet. When the time came for me to leave to go to New York, he pulled out this file that had my name on it. Now every morning they'd cook breakfast. Bacon and eggs, things like that, and they'd give you one hot biscuit, as his wife made biscuits. Now if I ordered another biscuit any time, Wilbur wrote down to charge me ten cents. So as I came to leave he had this bill all made out for me: "You owe me so much for biscuits, so much for an extra egg on this day or that day..."

Now as I was working for him at the theater, he took out what I owed him from my pay. I got disgusted with that. But Wilbur never changed. I went to Africa and Europe with him years later, but he never was any different, always wanted everything for himself.

So when I got back to New York, I went with a bandleader named Lou Henry. He had a ten-piece band playing theaters on the circuit with acts. In those days the bands that backed theater acts were very good bands. It doesn't mean too much today, but they were the thing then. We travelled round the circuit out East, playing with Lou Henry. Then he brought in a director by the name of Lieutenant Tim Brymn. He had been with Jim Europe's band in Europe, and was a fine musician and conductor. He knew his music from A to Z. I stayed with the band for about a month. We had a little revue like a Cotton Club show with chorus girls, comedians and everything.

Playing shows, Broadway shows and so forth never really interested me. I subbed every so often, but I'd start to drop off to sleep in the pit waiting for this cue and that cue. I really only worked in theaters a couple more times after that revue, and very much later in my career. I was involved in a Cavalcade of Jazz that Ed Sullivan put on in a Broadway theater, an all-black affair. But it didn't work out. And then I played in a little band on stage for Alfred Fontaine in "The Pirate". That's about the extent of my Broadway showbiz career. It never moved me. Of course it's security, and one of the best jobs a musician can have, along with studio work, because you know you can live the way you want. With that kind of work you could buy a home, a car, move out of the ghettoes and out to Long Island or somewhere. Like a lot of other New York work, it was cliquey, the same contractors hiring the same groups of good musicians all the time. Even in the 1920s I

21

didn't want that. I wanted to be free to come and go and play what I wanted to play.

In the late '30s, I had the chance to work with Noble Sissle down at the Diamond Horseshoe. I went down there to see what was going on, and Sissle worked those musicians like they were dogs! He wouldn't let them hardly take a breath, and so I cut out from there right away. Eubie Blake, on the other hand, who did all those shows with Sissle, was a great great man, and he and I got on fine together. He'd come down from time to time to see me where I was playing. Right up to his old age he'd come over between sets, and sit and talk, laughing and carrying on. He told me once: "Doc, I never had a glass of water in my whole life. I drink wine. When I was drinking seriously I drank other stuff but never water."

I said, "What do you mean by that?"

He said, "I've lived as long as I have on account of I never had a glass of water in my life!"

He was a grand old man. I remember going to his rehearsal in New York one time when he was leading an orchestra. He was still young in those days, a big, buxom, heavy, strong-looking cat, who always stood up very straight, very erect. I sat out in the audience as he rehearsed. A friend of mine I knew from Bobby Lee's band called Joe Hayman, a saxophonist who later became a pharmacist, was playing lead in the band, and he was by that time also a very famous soloist who'd worked with Claude Hopkins and Josephine Baker.

They were playing some charts by Eubie, and they got down to the last number, and as they made the ending for the final time, Joe deliberately blew a 7th on the last chord, which wasn't written. I thought it sounded beautiful. But Eubie wasn't having any of it. He jumped right up and shouted: "Who the hell was that, playing that 7th on the last chord?"

He wanted to fire whoever did it. I knew right away who it was, but Joe kept quiet, and Eubie clearly hadn't worked out who it was. Back then, which I guess was in the '20s, people really didn't play those chords on endings, and that was why Eubie was wild.

After I finished with Lou Henry, I played a couple of gigs with Chick Webb's band. That was the first time I met Johnny Hodges and Freddy Jenkins, who were with him also. Chick was just as sensational a drummer in the mid-twenties as he became later on. People didn't understand at the time how good he was. He didn't really become famous until later years, when Benny Goodman and Gene Krupa started running up there to the Savoy to hear him. I'm pretty sure he was at the Savoy in the twenties when I first heard him. At that time he had Charlie Holmes alongside Johnny Hodges in the saxes, and they both sounded just alike. There was no difference between the two of them.

I'd met many of Chick's band at the Rhythm Club, which was a musicians' club here in New York where musicians would go during the daytime and hang out when we weren't working. It was at 168 West 132nd Street, and all the black musicians in town (it wasn't a club for whites) would play cards, shoot pool, and talk. People would call up the Rhythm Club if they wanted a band for some function or another, and bands would be put together there and then. We had a great fraternity-like thing going on there. Some years later, the club went to pot, and moved, then it closed and the musicians had nowhere to fraternise. That's the way it is today, nowhere to go and meet one another, sit down and have a drink, or eat, and discuss old times.

Chick used to go down to the club a lot. He wasn't the kind of band director that stood out in front of the band with a baton. His drums were set back, on an elevated platform. From there he could look down at the music the trumpets and the saxes had in front of them. He mainly concentrated on the trumpets, and from his drums he would play every riff, every important phrase the trumpets would have, and underline it in rhythm. He was the first one ever to do that. Chick was a guy who could come by the club, or stand on the street corner and talk, but he knew every musician in his band, how he played and what he sounded like. He used to sit there and hum solo choruses in the style of all the musicians in his band. He loved to do that, and mimic all their styles. Before he joined the band, Chick could imitate Jimmy Harrison on trombone. Just as I don't think he was really given the credit for

23

what he did on drums, I don't think people realise just what a great band director he was. To know that, you'd have to know him like we knew him, meet him on the street corners in Harlem every day, and talk for hours. He talked nothing but music, arrangements, soloists. He could hum complete arrangements down from top to bottom, and put in all the solos. A lot of the schools I go to today, where the kids are learning about music, don't teach them anything about the great old-time pioneers like Chick. I think it's a pity that he has to be forgotten, because it was those pioneers that got us to where we are today.

It's hard for musicians today to understand what it was like in the '20s. There were all kinds of bands playing all over New York, specially up in Harlem. All kinds of players had the opportunity to express themselves on their horns. You'd all be playing the arrangements, trumpet players standing up on the bandstand waving their derby mutes together, but all the time we were creating. It was new, exciting and vital.

That's what guys like Edgar Sampson did for Chick Webb. They wrote new stuff that was never played before. And because all the great bands, Chick's, Tiny Bradshaw's, Lucky Millinder's, were working every night, all that new music got played. Many musicians got a chance to play new things, too. Today's atmosphere is so different it's hard to understand what it used to be like. Now you have to rely on a few festivals, and most of the musicians are choice musicians that they invite. So there's little chance for young musicians to come up and get a chance to show what they can do, working in an everyday band. I guess we have to take our hats off to the mafia for making what went on in the old days possible. They kept everybody working, money was no object, and they didn't give a damn. Nowadays if somebody has a restaurant, the most they'll bring in is piano, bass and drums and there'll be no money left over for a couple of horns. In that climate there's a division of styles as well that didn't happen in the old days. Places that'll hire musician A won't hire musician B, and I think that's a shame. In the old days when everybody was playing at the Savoy, and Smalls' and all those other clubs, everybody had a chance, and we developed some great players, because all those clubs had great bands.

I had pretty much made up my mind to join Chick's band when I played a dance somewhere downtown, and that's when Sam Wooding sent for me and I ended up going to Europe myself, playing lead trumpet in Sam Wooding's band. When I joined Bobby Lee's band I had begun to play lead trumpet for the first time. Now before I joined, Sidney De Paris had played with Bobby Lee, so when Wilbur wanted someone to work alongside Sidney, naturally he thought of me. He wanted me to play lead, so I did, and that was the beginning. I was branded. Right up until after I joined Cab Calloway, no-one ever knew I could take a solo, because I never had the opportunity to play a solo in any of those bands. I played all Tommy Ladnier's solos after he left Sam Wooding. I could do that. I had no trouble. But no-one knew that, and I think I lost a lot of work in later years because guys in New York refused to hire me. They'd say to themselves; "Oh, he's a lead trumpeter. He can't play solos."

When I met Sam Wooding, he'd already come back from Europe the first time. He was a great, great musician. His father was a doctor from Pennsylvania, and Sam himself was a graduate of a music school down in Philadelphia. He knew his music up here and down there, but he didn't know a thing about jazz. He knew a lot of classical things. There was nothing you could ask him about classical music he couldn't tell you.

I met him in 1927, when his band was going through a big change. He'd played piano himself up to that point, but he brought in Freddy Johnson to play piano for him, which made a big difference. Three or four of the other guys wanted to stay in New York, so for the next tour of Europe, he hired me, Jerry Blake, a guy name of Burns on trombone and Ted Fields on drums.

When Sam first asked me to join I said I wouldn't take the job unless he took Jerry Blake along too. And Sam was glad that he did, because one of the other big changes we made to the band, as well as new players, was bringing in new arrangements. We had a different type of arranger, more modern, than Sam had had before. Jerry Blake was a very fine arranger and he did a lot for the band. We played a lot of his pieces, and most of the real good ones the band played were his. He had a little hand organ that fitted in a carrying case, and had a little detachable pedal to pump it. Following Jerry's example, I bought one too, to run over chords and things. When we travelled together, Jerry and I would set up the organ in a hotel room to practise, and to help him with his arranging. I didn't know anything about arranging, but I made one arrangement for Sam that he recorded in Europe, called "Carrie", but it took me almost a year to make it. That wasn't my kick. My kick was learning. That's all I wanted to do.

Of course the band had some very fine soloists. I'd heard about his star trumpeter Tommy Ladnier before I joined. I was very happy that he was there because I wanted to learn more about jazz and the New Orleans type of jazz in particular. I knew quite a lot already, because I'd spent two years in Chicago, on and off, but to me Tommy was like the second Louis Armstrong, and he had a lot to tell me and to teach me. And he did. I watched him playing and the things he did and I learned a lot from that, but I roomed with him too and learned a lot more from him. We talked about how a man should feel when he's playing. I didn't want to be just a mechanical trumpet player, copying another guy's style, because I think that's wrong. Everyone should have their own style. I used to play flat footed - that is I never would pat my foot. Tommy would get on to me and say, "Doc! Pat your foot! You never can play jazz flat footed." I've always remembered that.

If you ever got the chance to listen to King Oliver, you could tell where Louis got his influence from. Tommy Ladnier also. You could tell where Tommy got his influence from.

I think Tommy was in a class by himself. He had a different way of expressing New Orleans style, but you could tell he was from New Orleans. Red Allen, too. You could tell Red was from New Orleans. You could tell a lot of those guys. They had something going among themselves. Maybe it's the climate or something, but they were all great down there. Every one was great, and you could tell their playing apart from the guys out of St. Louis like Charlie Creath. I met all of them, like Charlie, who worked on the Mississippi boats, but they had a different way of expressing themselves on the trumpet. They didn't have the soul

26

the New Orleans players had. Of course Louis himself worked on the Streckfus lines, and so did Shirley Clay. Shirley was an exceptional jazzman. He somehow caught on to some of the New Orleans style of playing very quickly. As I've said before, he worked with Louis at the Sunset in Chicago as a sideman in the band and he got hold of some of the ideas. I think it was very difficult to get that New Orleans idea of playing, it's something that you have to be born with, and though a lot of players tried, they never succeeded in getting that certain inner feeling in whatever you play that gives you the flavour of New Orleans.

Shirley Clay and I became great buddies. That was years after Sam Wooding, when we were working the dancing schools here in New York. He and I would get together, and it was a very different thing from when I roomed with Tommy Ladnier. I think Shirley's the only trumpet player I've ever known where we'd get together and rehearse. We used to do our vibrato like Louis did. And that was all wild practise - shaking our heads and holding the tune, or bringing our heads up and down while we held a note. But that's what Louis did. That was his vibrato in those days.

That's a funny thing, that kind of vibrato that Louis had. I remember once in New York, they have an annual brass conference at the Roosevelt Hotel. It lasts about a week, and my good friend Jimmy Maxwell was making a speech about vibratos, and he named all the vibratos but the head vibrato. After his speech I met him, and I said, "Jimmy, you did very good up there, but you forgot about the head vibrato." And he laughed about it because he thought it was something just New Orleans musicians did; most all of them got that vibrato from the head, not the lip. Other players have a lip vibrato, or a diaphragm vibrato, or a hand vibrato from moving their hand back and forwards, but Jimmy really didn't know anything about the head vibrato, so we had a good laugh about that. Of course, Louis sang with a head vibrato, too. He would sing: "Oh Yeah-eh-eh-eh!" That's just the same way he played back in those far off days. He had a good hand vibrato too, especially when he was playing fast.

But back to Sam Wooding. We had a terrific band. It wasn't one of those corny old bands, we had a hell of a band. The people

27

really liked it.

The boat docked at Cherbourg, and we took the boat train to Berlin. Berlin became the headquarters of the band, and we stayed in a *pension* at 28 Ranka Strasse. To me, Berlin was a most beautiful city. Each day I used to ride on top of the bus down the Unter den Linden with trees overlapping the street. I was never so happy anywhere as while we were there. They treated us like kings.

From Berlin we travelled all over Europe. I guess the furthest flung place we went to was Istanbul (they called it Constantinople then) but we went all over Germany, Romania, Czechoslovakia, Holland, France, Spain and Belgium. In about every country all over Europe, Sam was recognized as having one of the greatest entertaining bands in the world at the time.

When we set off first, we had a show called the Chocolate Kiddies. We had some girls and a singer, Edith Wilson, and a dancing act. But we played in Darmstadt, and after that he discarded the show. For the rest of the year we travelled with just the band, in fact for the rest of the entire time I was in Europe. This was mainly because we had a lot of single engagements where they didn't want singers, dancers and entertainment, just the band.

Every one of the members of the band had a feature. I played "Sweet Lorraine". I'd play it from the back of the theater and walk down the aisle playing the melody, and come up on to the stage. I didn't sing then, just played, except for a couple of things where we had a singing chorus like a glee club, and we did a few of those together. But I was responsible for the lead trumpet playing of the band so I didn't do too much of anything else but that.

Tommy played all the solos. He played all the second trumpet parts too, but he had a solo on just about everything. Gene Sedric, who played tenor saxophone with us, was another great, great player. During that time he was considered to be someone like Coleman Hawkins. He did a lot of writing for Sam's band, and he was a good arranger. We never worked together again, because he went with Fats Waller, and I eventually joined

McKinney's Cotton Pickers.

While I was with Sam, we made some records in Barcelona. In those days they recorded straight onto wax discs, but it was so hot that the wax began to melt as we were recording. So they had to put ice on top of the wax while we recorded, to prevent it from melting. Because of this, we stayed there a long time. We ended up being there just about all day trying to record. It was a very hard thing.

The bass player with Sam was called Edwards - "King" Edwards - and he was great on tuba and string bass. He was very elegant, very "British" to look at. He stood upright, very erect and proper. But off the bandstand he'd be very active. By the end of a long dance he was usually high. By the time we got to our hotel he'd usually be out of it completely. So we all used to leave our shoes and washing outside his door when we were on the road. They'd shine the shoes and wash the clothes, and all the costs would go on his room.

Ted Fields played drums alongside Edwards, and the main thing I remember about Fields, as well as the fact he played great drums, was that he always played standing up.

Tommy left the band while we were in Nice, France. Our gig in Nice was at the Hotel Negresco, and it was a great one. Once a week we played for a gala night at the Hotel, where there'd be visiting nobility like the Prince of Wales or the King of Norway. The band used to have a special table near the bandstand where we were waited on through the night with food, drinks, special Turkish coffee, and just about anything else we wanted. In the daytime, I used to go across to the beach opposite the Hotel, swimming and thanking God that I was there. I was sad to see Tommy go, when he left us to join Benny Peyton at the Casino Med. But I was happy to get his solos!

After Tommy left, I roomed with Sam as we were both cigar smokers. I always went to bed early. Sam would usually come in late, and after reading for a while in bed, he would reach for a cigar which he kept next to the bed. One night the cigar was missing. Sam raised hell, and accused everyone but me. I did take it though, and I smoked it then and there because it was the last cigar in town. I never told him about it until years later, but whenever I saw him after that we always had a good laugh about it.

The band was very well dressed always. Sam bought a very large dog-walking suit and the rest of the guys in the band promptly dressed the same. Few of us cut as fine a figure as Sam himself, who was very well respected, and pretty much kept himself to himself. He used to walk along the boulevards with his dog and (when she was travelling with us) his wife on his arm too.

On the way back from Turkey, we rode third class on a train to Hamburg. It was a two day trip, stopping at every little place. The train was so slow, we could get out and walk beside it, eating hot dogs at each small stop. The train got completely full of people, taking up every compartment. We wanted to be left alone, so when the train stopped to pick up people, they'd peer into our compartment. We would jump up and down and do a wild dance to scare them away, in order to keep them out.

In Hamburg, Jerry Blake and I decided to leave the band. Sam wasn't paying us as much as the other guys in the band, so we loaded up our trunks onto a truck and headed for the railroad station. But someone must have seen us and told Sam, because he came and brought us back to the hotel. So we returned to the band, and stayed until 1930 during the stock market crash, when the band was at the Paris Club Florida.

I recorded with the band in Paris, as well as being on those earlier records from Spain. But there was a big difference for the band, living in Paris rather than Berlin. I really couldn't catch on to Paris at that time. The people were so different. When I got back to the US I was sorry for a while that I'd left Europe, and I guess I'm still in love with Europe somehow. Although it has changed a lot, as everywhere has since the '20s, I met some beautiful people and musicians during the time we were there.

At various times in Paris I saw Josephine Baker perform there, but I never met her. In fact I knew many of the entertainers in Paris including Bricktop and Valaida Snow. I knew them, but they didn't know me. I'm an onlooker. I stay away back and see them operating. But I never was a society-going cat and I stayed in my place all the time. I never pushed myself to meet anybody.

From Sam's band I went back to the United States. I gave in my notice because I wanted to play a better type of jazz. Sam Wooding's band was a great jazz band, but I wanted to go higher. I arrived in New York City, went by the Savoy, and there was Marion Hardy's band, the same band I left Nashville with, but with two different men, of course. They were sounding good and offered me a job, so I joined them. They took me straight to Chicago where the headquarters of the band was. So we did one night stands, five, six or eight hundred miles every night, jumping all over the United States.

The band was good but I wasn't quite satisfied. Then I had an offer to go with McKinney's Cotton Pickers, which I jumped at because they were one of my favourite bands. In fact I'd heard them before, shortly after I got to Chicago with Marion Hardy's band, on a radio broadcast from the Greystone Ballroom in Detroit. I can't remember who it was in the band had this radio, because I didn't have a radio myself at the time, but I heard them, and I knew that was the band I wanted to play with. I wanted that very badly, they were the only band I'd heard that I really liked. So I said to myself, "Someday I hope to be able to play with that band." And I did.

Benny Carter joined the band at the same time I did. He replaced Don Redman as the musical director and conductor, and he took me with him, because there were no other lead trumpet players around New York. Everyone else wanted to be a soloist. I didn't know one that wanted to be lead horn.

With McKinney, Rex Stewart, Joe Smith and myself were the trumpet players. They had Quentin Jackson on trombone and Cuffee, I never knew his real name but we called him Cuffee, also on trombone. The saxophone players were Ed Inge, Prince Robinson, Jimmy Dudley, and then there was Dave Wilborn on guitar, Cuba Austin on drums and Billy Taylor, bass. He was playing tuba then though he later went on to play string bass with Fats Waller and Duke Ellington.

Rex Stewart was a very nice fellow. His playing was unorthodox, and nobody else could figure out how he played the

31

trumpet like he did. In fact, he was playing cornet rather than trumpet. He was a very fine man. I was with the Cotton Pickers maybe a year and I stayed until things got bad. McKinney had no money and we weren't getting paid. Then Billy Tayor left and took all McKinney's music, and held it until he'd been paid. That was enough for me and Benny Carter, and we quit at the same time. The band broke up for a while as he reorganized. I got a telegram to come to the Cotton Club in New York and see Cab Calloway and so I came straight to New York and ended up joining Cab Calloway's band.

One thing I remember most about the Cotton Pickers was the rhythm. Today, there's no more rhythm sections around. In fact, rhythm sections should be called "solo sections at the back", because you don't have rhythm today. Everyone's a soloist. Guitars - they've learned to be great soloists. Piano players - why, they're running all over the piano and they're soloists, too. Bass players are playing like flutes, and there's no bass there any more. Then there are the drummers. Every one of these drummers is so great they want to show off all they know. So when a guy's out front playing a solo, you hear all that confusion in the back instead of that solid, solid rhythm you used to hear years ago.

Just listen to the Cotton Pickers to hear what I mean. Any time there's a soloist or a vocal, it sounds as if the whole band stops playing and you can hear the solo or the words. Don Redman insisted on that and he got it.

There's no other band in the world like McKinney's Cotton Pickers when it comes to discipline and respect for singers and soloists. If I were ever to have my own private Hall of Fame the drummer I'd put in would be Cuba Austin. Most of the time you wouldn't know Cuba was sitting back there. You wouldn't know he was on the stage. But what time he had! He'd get his foot going right and the band would just swing. He had a box of hats and he would throw those hats in the air while he was playing. He could get them flying in the air, and then one would land on his head right on the beat: "Bam!". That was real originality. Cuba chewed tobacco and after a week at the Roseland, there'd be tobacco running all over the bandstand. He stayed out of everybody's way and you never heard him banging or carrying on behind people. But that's what's happening nowadays. All over Europe and everywhere, drummers have gotten so loud. They get those big heavy sticks and they're sweating like bulls, but it's all so unnecessary. When a guy's playing a solo, why drown him out banging on the cymbals? And do you have to have all those backgrounds if you're trying to sing? Listen to the Cotton Pickers and hear how Don Redman, and later Benny Carter, put that band in a very quiet position, how they'd drop right down when anybody was singing.

Of course you've got one or two drummers around today that I know who I'd add to my Hall of Fame. I have one now in my Quartet by the name of Jackie Williams. He's so well thought of that everybody's raring to get Jackie to go here, there and everywhere, because you so seldom hear solid rhythm, solid background, any more.

The Cotton Pickers were so perfect, there were almost no changes from night to night. Everyone in the band loved it and the arrangements we played. We had great respect for one another, and to some of the band it was their whole life - Dave Wilborn lived and died for that band. Sometimes people ask me 'Who's your favourite trumpet player?' I think it's wrong to ask me that, because every trumpet player I've ever heard is my favourite, because they all have something different from one another. But I always mention Louis first, because no-one in our lifetimes was as great as him. I don't want to compare him with nobody. But I did meet one trumpeter when I was in Detroit with McKinney's that you never hear anything about. His name was John Nesbit. John was a creator. He created those screams, those out-chorus high note screams that the bands all do now. He created that with the Cotton Pickers, those out-choruses where the trumpets all go up in the stratosphere. He created that, but he isn't given any credit for it.

4
With Cab Calloway

Playing with Cab Calloway was what I'd call my first "first class" job. We got paid every week, travelled in the best buses, slept on Pullman cars - in other words we lived like kings. I joined Cab in 1931, and stayed until 1939. We were at the Cotton Club, replacing Duke Ellington once a year. Duke'd go out on the road and we'd come in to the Cotton Club. Then when we went on the road Duke would come back into the club. It was like that.

The hours at the Cotton Club were really long. We'd have to be there every night at 7.30. We played for dancing up until about 8.30 when the show came on and then we'd play sometimes up until four o'clock in the morning. If the house had a lot of people we had to go on beyond four, and we'd end up doing four shows a night. Of course we were playing other jobs, theaters and so on, in the daytime. We might play five or six shows a day in a theater out on Long Island, or in Brooklyn, all around those places. So on a really punishing day I'd be playing maybe ten hours altogether, which was pretty good for the lip - or pretty bad for it! I was lucky, I never had much trouble with lip.

The owners of the Cotton Club weren't tight with money. They didn't care, they had the money to hire the best entertainers they could get. Bill Robinson, Adelaide Hall, people like that. There'd be Ada Ward and the Cotton Club Boys. Usually they had a pianist and a singer that did the songs there between sets. It would take me a long time to remember all the acts that worked there, as they changed the show about every month. They had all those beautiful showgirls, all those chorus girls. It was spectacular.

Once in a while, like election day, they'd have Cab play for the President or the Mayor. One time some gangsters had us take the whole Cotton Club revue to Sing Sing, and we played inside the prison, because one of the mob was in there and they wanted to provide some entertainment. We took the band, the girls, everybody and put on the full show for them in the prison.

Cab was so famous that he was booked to play most of the large theaters in New York at one time or another. A theater show would start at 8am. In some there was no time to sleep, and we'd be playing five or six shows a day. We used to set up army cots down in the basement, rush down there between sets to grab 15 minutes of sleep, and then go right back on stage again.

We used to broadcast from the Cotton Club. When this was going on, we were on air every night. Cab already had famous writers and arrangers producing material for the band, like Harold Arlen, Cole Porter and Irving Mills. But the radio drew hordes of little guys that were trying to make it as songwriters, and they'd come and wait backstage every night, or they'd come to a theater where we were playing and stand out there all day hoping to sell Cab their new tunes. Walter Thomas was the band's main arranger when I joined, but Cab also used Eddie Barefield, Benny Carter, Fletcher Henderson and a whole lot of strange arrangers I'd never heard of, like Billie Holiday's father Clarence, who wrote some things for us. We had so many arrangements coming in all the time, because we were expected to play new things on the radio.

When we went on the road, Cab was booked in all directions. Irving Mills was his designated agent, but the mob set up everything. One of them was always around. You didn't hardly know it. If you didn't know him, then you wouldn't know who he was. Of course Cab made big money then. I never saw so much money in my life. They couldn't find places large enough to accommodate Cab Calloway and the band. So they had tents, warehouses, tobacco warehouses. places like that. He was truly sensational - the greatest thing that happened in this country during the depression. He was on the radio, and he made all those Betty Boop films and things, and the people wanted to see him everywhere.

Once we were playing a one night stand in one of those tobacco warehouses. When we finished, we were all gathering outside. Somebody spotted this guy walking in the grounds of the place around the back, looking suspicious, as if he wanted to hold somebody up. He must have known that we were going to bring the receipts out of there. As he turned, Andy Brown hit him on the head with a Coca-Cola bottle. He clocked him right on top of the head, and that was the end of that. But then we had to get the money out, that all those people had paid to see us. We had to wrap it all in bed sheets, and stuff it into our instrument cases, because we had to get it across town to our Pullman car. So we helped Cab by opening all our cases and taking the heads off the drums, just to hide the money in something.

With all that money, the band looked really sharp. We had beautiful uniforms and we could change uniforms twice a day. There were two band valets, Harold and Rudolph. They saw that everything was set up in the dressing rooms at the theaters, saw the bandstand was set up, they dressed Cab, valeted for Cab, things like that. Working for Cab as a valet was hard, and he'd had several other valets who'd taken to drink and burned themselves out in the days before Harold and Rudolph. We used to take our horns with us, but they looked after the bass and the drums, and made sure everything was in its proper place when we went on stage. Leroy Maxey, our drummer, copied a lot after Sonny Greer, who played with Ellington. He had the same outfit Greer had, with big beautiful chimes in the back and a whole shiny new set of drums. I guess there was a little competition there between the bands.

Our band was given instruments by different makers, keen to promote their products. Selmer gave away saxes, Vincent Bach gave me a horn. Buescher and the others all came round. Vincent Bach would bring a whole set of instruments, trumpets and trombones, down to the Cotton Club and give them to the guys to try. He had little signs made saying "as used by Cab Calloway". The guy from Jet-tone, Ratzenburger, would bring mouthpieces round. Once he persuaded the band to try out a whole new set. That was tough, expecting the whole band to alter their embouchures to try new mouthpieces on the job, but we did it.

Travelling by Pullman was much better than the way some other bands travelled. We had our own special Pullman, and all the band, the dancers from the show, the comedians, all travelled together. We'd go to bed on the train after the show, and wake up where we were playing next - they'd shunt the car into a side track and there we'd be. Once Cab had set up his little office on the train and he was paying us. There were piles of money, and he paid me first. Then he paid all the other guys and I heard him calling, "Doc! Doc Cheatham! Don't you want to be paid?"

And he paid me again. I didn't tell him about that for nearly 50 years, but it was one of the only times I saw Cab make a mistake with money.

I guess there are a lot of stories about black musicians travelling through the South on buses, old broken-down buses, doing one night stands. The stories have been told so many times they may not seem important, but they were to us. Before I hit the big time with Cab, I travelled on buses called Newark Buses out of Newark, New Jersey, and sometimes they broke down before we got where we were going. When we travelled through the South we had to sleep on the bus. Every musician did this, in bands like the Cotton Pickers, the Alabamans and so on. We had single seats, and we had our pajamas. We'd hang our pajamas over our seats. We had to change our clothes on the bus, too. After the job, we'd get to the bus, change into our pajamas, hang our suits up, and when we woke up the next morning we'd dress on the bus.

And it was no use worrying about getting something to eat out there, because you couldn't eat in white folks' restaurants. You could stop, and draw the bus round the back; or stop two or three blocks away and send the manager. We always had a manager who travelled with the band. Sometimes the manager was white, but white or black, he'd take orders from the guys and go round to the restaurant, fix the food, and bring it back on to the bus to give to the guys to eat. Sometimes they had to eat things they didn't want or like. Other times there was no menu to pick from and you took what you were given. But we were lucky to get anything to eat out there.

I remember once, we were with Cab Calloway on the Pullman car, and we woke up this particular day on a side track. We were in the town where we were playing that night. We looked out of the window, and there, across the street was a restaurant. A white restaurant. Now Claude Jones, our

37

trombonist, could pass for white anywhere, so he went on over by himself, sat up to the counter and they fed him. He was just getting started when Lammar Wright spied him. So he went in there too, because he thought it was all right. He sat down, but before he could order, the owner ran them both out of there, because he could tell straight away that Lammar wasn't white. Claude Jones got really upset, because he hadn't finished his breakfast.

But with Cab it was a lot of fun. Not like the old days on the bus, where sometimes we'd stop on the highway at a grocery store and stock up on cold cuts, milk and pies, things like that. That's what messed up most of our stomachs, because we had to eat things like that, travelling on the bus.

Of course, we would go to some towns where they had black restaurants. The minute we'd get there, they'd change the menu, and put all the prices up. So, for instance, where you could get a meal for 35 cents, they'd run it up to 75 cents because they knew we were coming. But we'd get good food in the black restaurants down there in the South. It was out of sight.

There was one restaurant in Atlanta, Georgia, run by a woman named Mom Sutton. All the musicians who travelled to Atlanta would stop by Mom Sutton's house. She had a long table, looked like it was a mile long, and she would serve everything that you could name. Sausages, bacon, ham, all kinds of eggs, hot biscuits, corn bread, white bread, light bread, homemade pies. And you could pitch absolutely to your whim, all for about 50 cents. Everyone we knew ate there.

There was a similar type of place near the Howard Theater in Washington. All the performers ate there at this long white table. There was one in Cincinnati, and also in New York, although you didn't have to worry about eating in New York. The place there was called Mom Bell's. She was a big, heavy, thick set woman, and she would bring great big huge baskets of food round to the back of the theater. She'd come up in the dresssing room every day and open these baskets. She'd have fried chicken, pork chops, ribs and homemade pies. She was a little more expensive, maybe 75 cents or a dollar for a meal, but that was very good for travelling musicians who'd come into town.

I guess there was always some place in every town where you didn't have to worry about food, but if we didn't find a black restaurant, we always did eat on the bus. We slept on it even more often, because there were so few black hotels available in the South that had room enough, and many of the ones that had room were just awful.

I went into one in Macon, Georgia, when I was with the Cotton Pickers band. It wasn't really a hotel at all, although there was a sign outside that said "Hotel". You went in and walked up some steps. Then you walked up even more steps, and there was no light. You'd get to a place where there's supposed to be restrooms, but it'd still be dark, and the stairs creaked. Finally, you walk into a room, and there's an old table there with a big old fat cat sitting on it and of course he's mad as hell.

Well finally we registered. The guy charged everybody maybe 50 cents, and gave everybody a baseball bat. I said, "What is this for?"

He said, "Well you might see some rats in your rooms, and they're often quite big ones, so keep this bat beside your bed at night."

It was true. Through the gaps and holes in the walls, you could catch sight of rats as big as dogs at night. And there were chinches and bed bugs all over the beds, which were filthy.

But we had to sleep there. What else were we going to do? We ended up sleeping in many places with rats, chinches, bed bugs, flies, fleas and mosquitos. You'd come back from a tour with bites all over your body and what they call crabs.

A lot of the black hotels were in that sort of condition. Once in while you ran into a very nice clean one, like in Charleston, Pittsburgh, or Cincinnati, but in most places you could bet on bugs. Up in Detroit, with the Cotton Pickers, we stayed in one of the nicest black hotels, but out on the road it was a different story. You'd go to the bathroom. Filthy. And you cannot imagine what the toilets were like. Never cleaned, everything on the floor, urine, smell and insects all over. We had a hell of a time, and it was an experience for us, but I look back on it now, and I wonder how in hell we put up with it. But we did, just to go to make those gigs and make people happy playing music.

We ran into some mean white people down there too, that didn't like us for anything. In Memphis, Tennessee, when I was there with Cab's band we started playing for an all white dance. The place was packed, but at the end people came up for autographs, running up all over the stage. That's what messed up everything. One white man objected to that so they started throwing things at the bandstand, bottles and everything. We had to hide under chairs, or pick them up to use as shields to prevent ourselves being killed. The riot got so bad we started throwing bottles back at them. Finally the cops came, and put us in a truck to run us back across town to the Pullman car. All the way across town as we were swaying in the back of the truck, people were throwing bricks at us and shouting. We got back to the Pullman, and next morning we were gone!

One day we played in Miami, Florida. I think it was the first time they ever had anything like Cab Calloway's band down there in Florida. The place was packed, and a lot of the people already knew Cab. They came to New York, they knew the Cotton Club, they knew the Mob and everything. Those people were great, but they'd also let some bad characters in there.

The bandstand was elevated, and I saw one of them come across the floor, look up at me, and call me down off the bandstand. I got down, and he gave me glass of corn whisky. I said, "I don't drink."

He said, "You're going to drink that!" It looked like he was going in his pocket for something, so I drank that glass of whisky straight down and went back on the bandstand. I'd only been back a short while when another guy comes over and throws a Coca-Cola bottle, and hits the drummer on the head. Knocked a hole in his head. It started getting pretty bad then, and they had to close it down and get the cops in to run everybody out. I never went back to Miami with Cab, although I have heard that the scene down there has changed a little.

It was very hard to play a white dance in the South without some kind of trouble going on. I was down there once with one of the other bands I worked with before Cab, and we'd played for four hours and were about to finish when a big old farmer came up to us. We stopped on time, and the guy said, "Play some more."

"No, we're finished, we've done our four hours," said the bandleader.

"I don't give a damn," said the farmer, who was drunk, "You're going to play, or I'm going to..." and he pulled out a pistol. Suddenly here comes another big cracker with a big juicy cigar in his mouth, drunk as well. He threw the cigar up on the stage and then jumped up himself and started to hit guys in the face, that sort of thing. So when that happens, it doesn't matter you've played your four hours and it's time to finish; you don't get paid for it, but you play. We ran into all kinds of problems like that and it got real dangerous. Eventually a lot of those Southern places got cancelled out by road bands, but until they did, it was just one of those things you had to go through with.

If you got sick out on the road, that was just too bad. Fortunately as we were mostly fairly young, none of the guys were very sick. So we didn't have too much trouble with that, only maybe some of them getting drunk. But if you did get sick it was too bad if you needed a doctor or anything. These days it's much better, you can be treated, eat in nice places, stay in good hotels, it's all a different scene. It's impossible to understand some parts of the black entertainer's life. Like the fear we had of going to Alabama. The feeling you got when the bus pulled into that state, or Mississippi, or Georgia, or Florida. The fear came over everybody in the band. But we knew we had to play. We had to work, to earn our living.

And they wanted us. But, in most of those places, they resented us too. Isn't that something? They wanted us to play, and then get the hell out of there. They did everything they could to harass us while we were there. A lot of musicians felt their whole lives had been hurt or damaged by going there. Others took it in their stride. One of those was Eddie Barefield.

We were in one Southern city, I don't remember which, but this was with Cab, and we had travelled to this particular place by bus. We were all on the bus getting ready to leave when two or three great, big, strong white crackers came up and got in the bus. Seemed like they wanted to beat us up, or something. We were lucky to have Eddie with us, because he took all three of them outside and took those cats on. He knocked all three of them out, and they were twice his size. Barefield was a bad son-of-a-gun, but a good man to have near, because nobody bothered us when he was around.

Old Ben Webster called him "Bull". Ben and Eddie were great friends - Eddie called him "Frog". Whenever they'd meet on the street they'd start wrestling and carrying on. I used to get so worried one of those guys was going to get hurt, but somehow it was always friendly.

One time we stayed in a nice hotel up in Buffalo. Everybody had single rooms, and after playing we all went up to go to bed. Early in the morning I was woken by someone knocking on Barefield's door.

"Bam! Bam! Bam! Bam!"
It kept on like that. I heard Eddie sleepily saying, "Yeah? Who is it?"

"This is Frog, Bull! Open the door!"

"Man, I'm asleep. You go on to sleep. I don't want to be bothered with you, at this time of night."

"Open the door, Bull!" Ben kept saying. "This is Frog talking. Open the door. And if you don't, I'm going to break it down."

It went on like this for some time. I got up and out of bed quietly as I didn't want Ben to see me peeping out of the door. He was swaying about out there, and he was high.

Suddenly "Bam! Boom!"

The door burst open and Barefield had jumped out of his room and he and Ben were wrestling all over the floor. The hotel had long curtains on the windows all the way down the hallway and tall ashtrays. As they wrestled, the curtains started falling, they knocked the ashtrays down, and still they wrestled this way and that. I started running along behind them, picking up the ashtrays and putting the curtains back up, trying to arrange everything before the manager could arrive and threaten to throw us out. Finally, they were still carrying on, so I got out of there. I flew out.

But it was all fun. That was the way Eddie and Ben were. Ben was usually high, and Eddie was sober, but that didn't make any difference. They were both strong, and if they met one another walking down the street they'd practically knock each other down just saying hello.

Ben Webster was a great man. And somehow or other he took a permanent liking to me when he joined the band. I don't know why. He always seemed to talk to me and show me things about my playing that nobody else did. One time I was in the dressing room practising "Sweet Lorraine". He came in and said "Doc, let me show you something beautiful on the bridge of that song." (Bridge is what we call the middle part of the tune.) He played something beautiful, and I play it now, every night, and think of old Ben. It was so beautiful I wrote it down, note for note. He often did things like that to help me. Later, he was responsible for me joining Teddy Wilson's band. They didn't need another trumpet player - they already had Harold Baker, Karl George, and a fellow named Prince, Gene Prince. But Ben pulled something and got me in that band.

Cab Calloway himself was a man that nobody could put anything over on. He was a very hip cat. I imagine he learned how to take care of himself out on the streets of Chicago. He knew all the tricks. I think one time we got him though, because as you know we always answered his lyrics. Whenever he'd sing: "Hi-de-hi-de ho!", we'd all say "Hi-de-hi-de ho!". We had to do that in just about all of his songs.

But there was one he did called "Kicking the Gong Around". I don't think Cab ever got hip to this, because the cats put something on him on that tune and he never said anything. Usually, when Cab heard something not going right, he'd turn right around and let you know that he knew exactly what was happening. But on that song, we did the same thing on every show, everywhere we went and got a little laugh, a little snigger, out of it. I guess his ears just weren't quite sharp enough to pick it up from way out in front of the band on stage.

He'd sing:

"Do you know Minnie?" And we'd sing:

"Yes, Minnie."

"She's tall and skinny!"

"Tall and skinny!"

"She gets ger pleasure, kicking the gong around." That's what the song was. So at the end of the song, Cab'd get to "Tall and skinny", so we'd sing it back. Then he'd sing:

"The curtain parted..." and every night we sang:

"And Minnie farted!"

Cab just carried straight on: "...and there stood Minnie, kicking the gong around!"

That's just about the only thing we ever did on stage. The rest of the time we were on our toes and did everything like it's supposed to be done.

Cab himself was one of the greatest bandleaders who ever lived. He had no worries about anything. He had that long white baton and he'd come out there and do his business.

In the days when we played theaters and we were doing so many shows, one right after the other, there was often only about ten or fifteen minutes between sets. We had no time to go anywhere, so we'd gather on stage behind the set while they were showing a short film. There was no time for a long picture between shows, but they'd put on a short, a comic film, something like that.

A lot of the guys liked to shoot craps, so they'd start a crap game back there. Cab would come down and get in the game. His valet, Harold, would be right there with him. He'd take Cab's jacket, his tie, his shirt and sometimes his pants, and Cab would get down to shooting craps. Cab always won. I never saw him lose. He'd have all the money piled up at the side because he'd be winning everybody's money. He'd loan a guy money from time to time, but he never forgot when he loaned money to someone.

After a while the call would come through from the theater management: "All on! Everybody! All on!"

We had to run and get on the stage, back on the bandstand. Meanwhile, Cab's valet went to work on him. He got his clothes

44

back on, combed his hair, and in a matter of minutes Cab would run out there on the stage, leaving all his money piled up beside the game. We'd do the show, a great show, like nothing was going on, but the minute the set ended they all went back there and carried on shooting craps and gambling again. Cab wouldn't ever lose a dime, and when the time came he'd gather up all that money, put it in his pocket and make his way back upstairs to his dressing room.

Up in our own dressing rooms, every man had a wardrobe trunk. When we arrived at a theater, we'd be assigned our dressing rooms. Usually each man had a room to himself. You'd go up there and your trunk would be there. You didn't have to do anything but open it. We had uniforms, like I said before, and they went from our neckties down to our shoes. We had jackets, socks, pants, shirts to change for every show. We had to wear a different uniform for each show when we were working a theater. You didn't even have to move your horn, although as I said, most of us preferred to carry our horns with us. We would leave everything in the dressing room, the valets would pick it all up, and you had no need to touch anything 'til the next date. When you got there, everything would be sitting ready for you in the dressing room. In many places there'd be a list at the stage door with everybody's name and the dressing room numbers. All you had to do was go up there, open up, get dressed and warm up your horn.

Old Lammar Wright was a great trumpet player, like me he specialized in playing lead trumpet. Playing with Cab didn't require great range, no very high playing, but Lammar used to play up as high as an *e* or an *f*, just for the novelty of it. His sons were both great trumpet players, too.

Old Lammar was a great chef. He bought one of those little portable electric cookers and he used to cook up in the dressing room. We used to smell that odor wafting downstairs from the dressing room, so everybody'd get hungry and go up there. He'd sell everybody a little plate of food for about a dollar a time.

He'd cook everything, chitlins, pig's feet and he'd make corn bread. Often this saved the guys from going out looking for food and anyway, the food we were getting on the road couldn't compare with the food old Lammar Wright would prepare for the band. Even Cab himself started going up and begging for Lammar's food. Lammar was very nice to me. Like everyone else in Cab's band he treated me very well and he was a great trumpet player.

When I first joined, Reuben Reeves was on first trumpet, but he and Cab had some kind of falling out or something. I don't know whether he was fired or if he just left, but I ended up taking over the first chair. I had no trouble playing the lead parts by then, because after touring with Sam Wooding I was pretty sharp. I could play anything and I didn't care what it was.

Mostly the solos were taken by Edwin Swayze and Lammar. I had ballads, one or two ballads, like "World on a String" and I played solos on them. Playing lead and a few ballads was enough for me. From time to time, perhaps, I played a few jazz solos, but you can't do that and play lead, it's too much of a strain. Swayze left, he died. Then Cab brought in Irving Randolph, who was a great trumpeter and he and Lammar did most of the work. Lammar covered most of the high playing, while Randolph took the jazz solos in there. I'd left by the time Mario Bauza and Dizzy joined the section. I left from the Cotton Club downtown in 1939, and Dizzy was there at the rehearsal. They were undecided about Dizzy, what he was doing, so they got another guy in to play lead, and they got Mario. He did a good job on lead. Dizzy wasn't interested in that anyway, but they joined the band at the same time.

When I first joined, the band was more or less just a show band for Cab, backing him all the time. He had a lot of stamina, but when he started to lose some of that, then he began to change the band. He felt he needed to take it easier, so he added one man at a time who were good soloists - Ben Webster, Shad Collins, Cozy Cole, Jonah Jones, Milt Hinton and Chu Berry. He had to change the band, because he knew he wouldn't be able to scream for the rest of his life.

The kind of work we did changed, too. We went to California with Cab and made pictures like "The Singing Kid". And we did the "Big Broadcast" with Bing Crosby. I figure we stayed out there about ten days at a time. It was very nice, we lived like kings out there. We made good money and everything was first class.

We went to Europe in 1934, but there the people didn't treat us the way we should have been treated. At that time, in New York, Cab was a sensation at the Cotton Club. I'm not taking anything away from Duke Ellington, he did a heck of job there, but the Hi-de-Ho man was the talk of the town. We came over on the S.S. Majestic and we were treated fantastically. People were so nice to Cab. He was asked if the band would like to play on the boat, and he agreed. We played quite a bit during the voyage. So it was a surprise when we opened up in London and the minute they announced Cab Calloway, all the musicians in the pit band blew loud discords and started making funny sounds on their horns. A welcome like that was embarrassing, for Cab and for us. But we did our act. I don't think the English audiences liked him at all. He was a screamer and a yeller, that's what made him famous, but that didn't go down well in England, and I don't think people even appreciated the fantastic band he'd brought with him. It was the same thing in Manchester, and although we were well received when we went to Scotland, we weren't the same sensation we had been in New York. I knew it. Cab knew it.

From England we went to Amsterdam, and the tour finished up in Paris. Cab was bitterly disappointed at our reception. At our last big concert in Paris he didn't show up for an hour after the show should have started. We sent the piano player to look for him, and when he found Cab, he was drunk. We brought him backstage to the dressing room, put a tub of black coffee into him and brought him back to some sort of life, but he was still drunk when he went on stage. This was very unusual, because normally Cab was a fanatic about discipline. But I think the tour had got to him, and he carried on terribly, trying to speak French. It was a shame because it was our one big concert in Paris and the place was packed.

In the last few years of his life, when Cab made a tour of Europe, there were lines waiting right around the block wherever he played. London, Paris, Norway, Japan, Cab was one of the biggest musical stars in the world. I would still get the biggest thrill when I ran into Cab, some place where I was travelling in Europe or in the USA. Once in a while we hooked up together for reunions, as I'm one of the few members of the horn section that worked with Cab still living. I made a recording with him a year or two ago, for Milt Hinton's birthday album "Old Man Time". Eddie Barefield and Milt and a few old members of the band were there, and we talked about old times. At that time, Cab was traveling with a little group, about nine musicians, they knew all of his music and they were very good.

I just have such a memory of that man. There isn't a night when I don't dream of Cab or the band. In my dream I'm always late, running down to the theater where they're playing. I dream about Cab more than anyone I've met in my whole life. I don't know why that is, but he was a great man. I loved that man, Cab Calloway.

5
After Cab

Even though I was playing lead trumpet with Cab, I had never had any formal trumpet lessons of any kind, I'd just learned the horn from watching others and playing. Now round about the middle of my time with Cab, the word was going around New York about this guy who was making sterling silver mouthpieces for trumpets and trombones that were really excellent. Talking to other brass players, that's about all you would hear, about this man whose name was Al Almont. You could wait there while he made them for you, it only took a few hours, so I decided to go up and visit him.

These things were selling like hot cakes, but I arranged to take my mouthpiece up there and for him to copy it. I sat there and waited until he had finished.

In the meantime, there was another man sitting opposite me in the big room outside the small workshop where Al Almont made his mouthpieces. I guess we were sitting in what amounted to a living room. The other guy was sitting there reading. Then Al finished my mouthpiece and he wanted me to try it, so he brought it out there into the living room, where this guy was sitting, and I played. The man turned to me and he said: "Who are you?"

I said, "I'm Doc Cheatham."

He asked, "Are you playing?"

"Yes," I said, "I'm on lead trumpet with Cab Calloway."

"Lead trumpet player?" he exclaimed, "Playing like that? Come over here!"

I thought to myself, "This guy is crazy!" But I walked over to him.

He said, "Now play something." So I played.

"You're going to kill yourself!" he said. "Playing like that!"

I said, "What are you talking about?"

"You're not blowing right."

"I've been a lead trumpet player for all these years and..."

"I don't care who you are," he said. "You're going to kill

49

yourself, because you're playing from your chest, and you should be playing from your diaphragm."

I said, "What's a diaphragm?"

So he moved over and sat on an upright chair next to me. I stood up in front of him and he put his hand on my stomach and said, "Now, play something!"

And my stomach didn't move.

"What the hell?" he said. "How can you do it?"

Then he told me to breathe naturally, put my own hand on my stomach, and then yell. I put my hand on my stomach and yelled: "Hey!" I felt my stomach pop back in. He said that was the same as when you yelled across the street at someone, when you holler, that's the diaphragm and you have to learn to control it, to breathe properly, and to take in the right amounts of air.

And so he taught me to breathe the proper way, without doing any damage to my lungs. He invited me back up there and I ended up going there several times. He wrote out some exercises for me, and I still have them and use them to this day. I stayed with him until he'd taught me exactly how to use my diaphragm, and it helped me tremendously.

I thank God he did.

At first I was worried that trying to change my way of playing and use my diaphragm would affect my lip. So I asked him.

"Nobody has ever lost their lip unless somebody cuts it off, or you bite it off," he said. And he showed me a great big chart on the wall with all the thousands of veins in the face.

"When you play tonight," he said, "all those veins in your lip will break. Then, when you go home, they'll heal while you sleep. That's the only trouble you'll have with your lip." I said I'd noticed feeling better after waking up, and that must be what it was.

Even after I'd been there a few times, I still didn't know who he was. He didn't tell me, so one of the times I went up there I finally asked him, "What's your name?"

He said, "My name is Schlosberg. Max Schlosberg."

I'd never heard of him, but I thanked him, and later on he gave me his book. I still have that, too, with all his exercises. He had me playing like nobody's business, with lip trills and all that. Another thing was playing long chromatic scales on one breath. I never knew anything about those things before, but it all helped me. He taught me for quite a time and never charged me a cent. He and his book are the things that have helped me most, all these years. Max Schlosberg. That's how I met him.

* * *

While I was still with Cab, I took sick on the bandstand of the Cotton Club downtown. I was worn out, through traveling and not eating right. I never was a drinker, I never drank anything, but I was thin during the whole nine years I worked with Cab. I went to the doctor, and he said, "I'll give you ten more years to live." The X-rays he had taken showed that I had a little scar on my lung, and it worried him.

That frightened me, and I went straight back to Nashville. My sister was by then a supervisor in the Hubbard Hospital there and she kept me in the hospital about four days. They did lots of tests, cleaning out the colon and all that stuff, but there didn't seem to be anything wrong with my lung. Finally my mother took me to the doctor that brought me into the world. He took one look at my X-rays, and he said, "Oh, that was on the X-ray when he was born."

So that was good news.

I stayed in Nashville about six to eight months. The doctors there said, "You should rest. Stay here. Don't worry. Stop playing for a while."

So that's what I did. I suppose I had had a little nervous breakdown, so I stopped playing music altogether. I stayed in Nashville about eight months, sitting out in the yard, eating and carrying on resting. Then, in the end, I drove back to New York, in an Oldsmobile I had at the time and when I got there Andy Brown approached me. He says, "I've opened this little studio. It's got two rooms, so why don't you take one of them, and you can teach people." I didn't have to pay him anything, so I took it.

Now around that time, I started to do some work with

Teddy Wilson's band, at the Golden Gate Ballroom. That was a beautiful place, with two bandstands, rather like the Savoy. Teddy Wilson's band was so great. It wasn't a hard-swinging band like some of those Savoy bands, exactly, but it had such great musicians in it it was really beautiful to play with. On the other bandstand they'd have Coleman Hawkins, or Andy Kirk: two bands every night. And it started to hurt the Savoy, or so I was told, and in the end, the Savoy people bought out the Golden Gate and closed it. Other rumours said that Benny Goodman had something to do with it too, and that it was because of him Teddy found it difficult to find work for the band after the Golden Gate closed, as Benny wanted Teddy to go back with him and Teddy didn't want to go.

I was so weak when I joined Teddy, after being ill, there was some discussion about what I was going to play. After all, in my condition I couldn't play lead, and I wasn't up to playing many solos as I just wasn't strong enough. So what Teddy did, out of the kindness of his heart, he wrote out a whole set of special parts for me, doubling up what the lead player would play, but an octave lower. That gave the band a special sound, a different sound, by doing that. Sometimes I felt Teddy wanted to fire me and get rid of me, after all, he had a perfectly good section with Harold Baker, Karl George and Gene Prince. But Ben Webster stood up for me. Like I said before, he had helped to get me into the band when I was in a very low state, and he pointed out to Teddy that now he'd written all these extra parts and the band's sound had changed we had something good that was worth keeping. In the end Teddy agreed, but I was very nervous all the time I was with that band because I was expecting to be fired. In fact, even after that, in every other band I played with I was expecting to be fired because I wasn't well. I was physically stronger, and I wasn't so thin, I was up to a hundred and ninety-something pounds, but I was so weak when it came to blowing that I played like a child. I had no power, no range, no strength or anything.

Harold Baker stood up for me, too. He amazed me, somehow, because he seemed to look up to me. Like I was really something. That's the way he treated me, and whenever we were playing together he'd see that I had a chance to play a little solo or something, after which he'd come over and shake my hand. Later on, when I was still with Latin bands, and hadn't really got back into playing jazz, he asked me to make an album with him for Prestige.

"Come on Doc," he said. "Let's do it with just the two of us playing trumpets and a rhythm section."

I don't really know to this day exactly why he picked me, but he insisted and he encouraged me all the way through the session.

I guess one conversation we had once gave me a clue as to why he was so good to me, and treated me so well, both with Teddy Wilson's band and later on.

He said, "You know one thing, Doc? You used to come through St. Louis with Cab's band when I was still a boy. There was a big place where you cats played that was like they used to have in old-time ball games, with rows of seats up on platforms. Well, I used to get underneath the platform, and sneak in there close to where you were all sitting on the bandstand and listen to the band all night long from real close by. And I thought you were great, one of the greatest trumpeters I ever heard. I liked to hear you playing lead, and to listen to your phrasing and tone and everything."

So I thought to myself, "That's where it all comes from."

There's nobody ever in the world played like Harold Baker, he was a great musician himself, but he was always respectful, kind and thoughtful to me. I don't think he should have used me on that session, I wasn't playing well enough. But what the heck. He did. And I feel very proud of him for that.

Teddy's band had some very fine musicians in it while I was playing for him. J.C. Heard was on drums, and then there was Rudy Powell on reeds along with Ben Webster, of course. When that band broke up I did a little work with Teddy Hill, and then I think I played a little with Lucky Millinder. I played with so many bands round that time, working at the Apollo Theatre or with other small groups, but my health was bad, and I still didn't seem to be making any money. After a while, I joined up again with

Benny Carter, but he seemed to be having trouble getting the band started. We played for a bit, made a few records, and then nothing. After that I had the chance to rehearse and play with Fletcher Henderson in what was one of the last bands he had. But he was ill and nothing really materialized.

Then I got a notice from the army to report for enlisting. They put me through all the examinations, and then they said they wanted to post me to the Philippines. There was this guy there, Russell Wooding, who had a band, and he was looking for a first trumpet player. "He asked us to look you up, and send you to the Philippines to join him."

I said, "Not me!"

"Well," said the man, "You have to do it."

"Listen," I said. "I'm thirty-nine. I don't have to go to the war, because my age is on the line."

"In that case, you have a choice," said the man. "You can either go to the Philippines, or, because of your age, you can go into some kind of service for the government."

So, I chose the United States Postal Service. I joined the S.I.S., that was a big complex out on Long Island where all the Army mail came. There were piles of it. Boxes and boxes, as well as all the broken boxes and packages that had to be sent to the correct place. And, of course, with the war on, there were all the things people were sending out to their relatives.

I went out there and stayed the best part of two years. During that time I didn't play a note. I pulled mail out of boxes, and I drove a jeep all round the complex dropping off sacks and boxes of mail here and there. I used to have to mend the broken boxes with tape, and patch up parcels that were coming apart, and then deliver them as well. I was still doing some teaching, but I didn't manage to play at all.

After a couple of years I was driving the jeep as usual, with about eight or ten loads of mail on the back. I was dropping this off, when the supervisor pulled me in.

"You're working too slow!" he said. "Put some pep in it!"

Well I was tired of the job anyway, and I'd done what I had to for war service, so I just dropped the jeep at the office and I told

54

Doc's parents, Marshall
and Alice Cheatham

Doc with his parents,
early 1930s

Pearl High School band: Doc (soprano sax) rear left, Jerry Blake (clarinet) front left

below left Bobby Lee and his Cotton Pickers, 1927, including Joe Hayman and Jerry Blake (saxes), Lincoln Mills and Doc Cheatham (trumpets), Juan Tizol (valve trombone) and Stafford (brass bass)

BOBBY LEE - PHILA- PA
AT SEA GERT INN- N-J. 1927

Doc in Europe
with Sam Wooding,
Biarritz, 1929

Doc and his mother, Chicago, 1930

below left
Cab Calloway's Cotton Club Orchestra, with Doc just to the right of Cab

Dinner at the Cheatham House, Nashville, 1932, with members of Cab's band. Left to right: Mrs Alice Cheatham (Doc's mother), Elma Turner (dancer), Eddie Barefield, De Priest Wheeler, Doc, Cab, Al Morgan, Marshall Cheatham (Doc's father, standing), Foots Thomas, Harry White, Mr Meredith, Morris White

With the Hi-De-Ho Man on stage

above right Doc Cheatham, lead trumpeter with Calloway

below left With Teddy Wilson's band, after leaving Cab. From left to right: J. C. Heard (drums), Harold "Shorty" Baker (trumpet), George Irish (tenor), Karl George (trumpet), Pete Clark (alto), Doc, Jake Wiley (face obscured, trombone), Rudy Powell (alto), Floyd "Stumpy" Brady (trombone)

below right Eddie Haywood, Café Society, with Lem Davis (alto), Jack "The Bear" Parker (drums), Eddie Haywood (piano), Doc, Vic Dickenson (trombone), Al Lucas (bass)

Doc, Wilbur De Paris, Omer Simeon, with De Paris's New New Orleans Jazz

above right Wilbur De Paris (left) and band being greeted by local musicians in Lagos; Doc, centre, with camera

below left With Herbie Mann in Kenya, 1960

below right The 1958 recording session with Juanita Hall. From left to right: Doc, Buster Bailey, Coleman Hawkins, Juanita Hall, Claude Hopkins, George Duvivier, Jimmy Crawford

A section of Machito's Orchestra. Back: left to right, Viva (drums), Doc, "Chocolati" (trumpet), Emilio Reales (trumpet), Chaparo (trumpet); front: Mario Bauza (clarinet/alto), Danny Turner (alto), Eddie Chamblee (tenor)

above right Doc's daughter, Alicia

Doc in Latin American guise with Ricardo Ray

Festival reunion: Doc and Vic
Dickenson with Major Holley (bass)

Doc and Phil Schaap celebrate
Doc's 80th birthday on air
(photograph: Nancy Miller Elliott)

Doc's New York Quartet: Bucky
Calabrese, Chuck Folds, Doc and
Jackie Williams at Sweet Basil
(photograph: Nancy Miller Elliott)

Doc and Nellie outside Sweet Basil
(photograph: Nancy Miller Elliott)

them: "I'm leaving." I took my papers and walked out.

After that I devoted my time just to teaching. I played a bit, after I left the Post Office, but not much. Harry Lim had a Sunday session at the Silver Slipper. It was a small club in the Village and I was there with Lester Young. Just the two of us played there with a rhythm section, and we were working as usual when Eddie Heywood came in looking for me. He listened for a bit, and then he hired me to join his Cafe Society gig. That was a great little band with Mary Lou Williams, Vic Dickenson, John Simmons, Lem Davis, and, of course, Billie Holiday on vocal. One of the other stars of that particular gig was Josh White. While I was there with Eddie we did some recordings for Commodore.

It was a great show at the Cafe Society Uptown. All the arrangements were done by Eddie, and at that stage he was still playing well, and had none of the problems with his hands he had in later years. Eddie talked with a stammer. He'd had it ever since I first knew him. Sometimes he could control it, but not when he got excited or nervous. When he was really relaxed he didn't stammer at all.

The band had a very small dressing room, which was too small and crowded for all of us. There was a lot of reefer smoking going on in there, but the band developed a perfect cover. They would sit me outside, smoking my pipe, so that the heavy smell of the pipe tobacco would cover up the scent of reefers, and stop it from drifting into the club. There was only one fight with Billie when I was there. Someone made a remark to her which she didn't like. The whole band flew into the room at once, and I ran out of the way!

It was a wonderful experience for me to be in that group, and Billie was always great to me, even though I was not her favorite trumpet player. She would have preferred Roy Eldridge or Buck Clayton, but she treated me very nicely all the same. On the bandstand she used to turn and smile at me. I was always standing on her left and I used to return her smile. One time she asked me to go over to her house for collard greens and chitlins, that sort of thing, but that's really as far as anything between us ever went.

When John Chilton was writing his book on Billie, he sent out a questionnaire with about 50 questions on it to musicians who'd known Billie. The last question was: "Did you love Billie?" I said I loved her so much I sometimes wanted to hit on her. Later I got a letter of thanks from John, and in it he asked: "But if you loved Billie so much, why would you have wanted to hit her?" He didn't know we used to use that phrase to mean to make it with somebody!

All this time I was teaching trumpet beginners at the studio I shared with Andy Brown. He'd told me I didn't need to pay him anything, unless business picked up and I had enough pupils to afford it. In due course I did. I had about sixty pupils, and most of them were doing pretty well.

One who wasn't was a kid who came there with his mother.

"I want you to teach my son to play trumpet," she said. I said I'd try, and she went out and bought him a trumpet.

He turned up for his lesson with a book with a picture of Dizzy Gillespie.

"That's what I want to play like," he said.

"How long d'you think it'll take him to learn?" asked his mother.

I replied, as politely as I could, "Madam, he may never learn how to play the trumpet with that attitude. The first thing he's got to learn is what the trumpet is all about, and start from the beginning."

"I don't want to learn no skills and stuff," he said. "I just want to play like this!" And he pointed to the picture of Dizzy. I told his mother to take him to somebody else.

6
The Latin Bands

I devoted my time to teaching until I came across a fellow named Marcellino Guerra. He was Cuban, and he came to me to learn the trumpet. He was already a bandleader, and he invited me to join his band. So, in the end I did, although when I'd tried playing with Machito one time, I was fired after the first night because the rhythm was too strange for me. With this smaller Latin band I seemed to catch on and I was hired. It was one of the best bands in town, with a mixture of black and Latin musicians.

I found myself sitting alongside another trumpeter called Hot Lips Garcia, who was a great Latin-Cuban player. I couldn't play lead in this band because I was still too weak on account of my illness, but they kept me in there for a long time until the band broke up. Then I went on to play with Perez Prado. He came through New York one time with a contract to play in South America, starting in Montevideo. He had a trumpet player named Fats Ford, who got mixed up in some trouble and the judge told him to leave town. So Perez Prado needed a trumpeter, and it seemed as though he always had trouble keeping good musicians. Later on I learned why - it was always to do with money - but someone had told him about me because I had recent experience playing with a Latin band.

So, I went down to his rehearsal and I joined the band. He needed another soloist, so I got Paul Webster to come down there, too, and he hired both of us. I'd known Paul for a long time. He and Jimmie Lunceford and Willie Smith, and some other musicians, Will Cox and a trombone player called Henry, they were all at Fisk, and they had a little group there. I first met Paul and Jimmie down there at the University when they were both at Fisk together.

When Paul worked with Jimmie Lunceford's band later on, he became one of the first great high-note jazz trumpeters. When we went down to the audition, Prado pulled out all those old tunes like *Cherry Blossom*. We played through them at the rehearsal and he liked the heck out of both of us. And I was starting to get stronger, something I had begun to think wouldn't happen. As I got my strength back, I started to play lead again, with Paul by my side taking the solos, two white trumpet players beside us, an all Cuban rhythm and one American saxophone player.

Once we started to work regularly I began playing solos, too. Paul Webster and I would go out to the front of the stand and trade solos: choruses, eights, fours - we tore up the place. Perez Prado would jump for joy.

We stayed down in Montevideo, then we went to Chile and all the time the money was slowing down. When pay day came, Prado was nowhere to be found. He'd make the job that night, but when we asked him when we'd get our money he always said "Tomorrow". When tomorrow came it was always the same old crap.

Finally we checked in to a hotel in Santiago, Chile. "Tomorrow," he told us, "I'll get the money and pay everybody off." We finished the job, and checked out of our hotel the next morning, got on to the band bus and set off for the airport with all our baggage and instruments and everything. We got about halfway to the airport when the motorcycle cops came after us and pulled us over. They made us take everything off the bus - the music, the instruments, the uniforms. There was even a sewing machine and needles and thread for mending the girls' costumes. They took that, too, and wouldn't let us leave town until our hotel bill had been paid. We thought Perez Prado had paid it, but he was hoping we'd all pay for ourselves. They took us back to the hotel, and somehow he got the money to settle the hotel bill. The Police hung on to our things until everything had been squared up, but even when it had, we musicians hadn't been paid.

Well, though I liked what I was doing with the band, I needed the money, because I'd decided to get married out there. We'd played a big concert in Punta del Este in Uruguay, and that's where I met my wife. I was out for a walk. I walk a lot, and I met her watering the lawn in front of her house. I stopped and talked to her there, and almost every day we were in town I went round there. We became very well acquainted, and I corresponded with her for about a year before I went back and we were married. People said to her 'Why do you want to marry an old man like that?' But in some ways she was living like a slave down there, you know. She was working herself to death, doing this and that for people with money. We fell in love with one another. I gave her the money to come to Santiago, Chile. But her mother locked her up in a room, and wouldn't let her out. So she started fasting, and when she began to starve, her health got very bad. So the doctors told her mother to let her go, and finally she made it to Santiago. She's a great wife. We have two children, a son and a daughter, and now they have two children each so I have four grandchildren. I was afraid that over time she'd change. Because women do change. They love the hell out of you but then things can change and get very uncomfortable a lot of times. But this girl of mine is just the same as when I married her!

She didn't speak English when I first met her, so I taught her, very slowly. And after I finally brought her back to New York, within six months she was speaking fluent English. Her accent was different, and some of the words she used, but she was speaking English, and in a year she was speaking really well. For much of the time we've been married, she's had a job as a courier, travelling between the USA and Argentina.

I never was a womanizer, never in my life. It always seemed funny to me, especially after playing all those concerts in Europe, girls would come up to you in the intermission with their autograph books, they'd look you in the eye and blink at you, but when the concert was finally over and you'd go out there, everyone's gone home leaving you looking like a fool. I was married three times, and the first two weren't successful, because I wasn't really prepared to settle down. The first time I was married, I was still with Marion Hardy. I shouldn't have done it, because one day I was married and the next I was gone. I tried very hard to settle, but I couldn't as the band were constantly travelling. So that marriage went on the rocks after about six years. The next time I married a very pretty girl who was in show business, as a chorus-dancer. I said to myself, "I'm in show

59

business and she's in show business, so this should be it." But it wasn't because once again I was gone on the road. So neither of my first two marriages worked out. I never had a family or any kids until I met my third wife in South America, and she's a dream. She has given me everything I never had out of marriage before. I can't move without she's doing this or that for me, and this is paying me off for all the miseries I had in my first two marriages.

So out there in South America, I needed the money I was supposed to be earning with Perez Prado. We made our way to Brazil and we were supposed to be opening in Rio. But he stopped on the way and played another job some place else, a different part of Brazil, on what should have been our opening night. When we got to Rio, of course, the manager of the place we were supposed to have played at said: "I don't want anything to do with you! Get out!"

We didn't get out, and Prado left us there in the theater rehearsing while the man was trying to close it up. What we were rehearsing for, I don't know.

We didn't get our money because of this, and so Paul and I called Prado and said "You owe us a few weeks' salary. What's going to happen?" He said we'd be going to Buenos Aires to play there and everyone would be paid.

So at that point, Paul and I said we wanted to be paid then and there, and we wouldn't go to Buenos Aires unless we were, because it'd just be the same thing all over again. Otherwise we'd quit at once. We went downtown and got a lawyer. The lawyer came and looked over our contracts which said we were supposed to be paid a salary in American money - dollars.

We got the lawyer to put a lein on the hotel so Prado couldn't touch the baggage or the instruments. In fact he wouldn't be able to play until we got paid. He got real angry with me and Paul because we got a lawyer, but he couldn't open in Buenos Aires without us because the people there had heard about the problem. They sent someone up to Rio to tell him that if he didn't bring those two boys on trumpet, his contract would be null and void. So he went downtown and got hold of the money, from Mexico or somewhere. When he came back, he called us to his

60

room. The money was on the bed, but it was Brazilian money, and our contract called for dollars. So he was up the creek, and we didn't take it, as our lawyer said we shouldn't touch it. In the end he had to go on the black market and get the money for Paul Webster and me. We got paid, and so did a trombone player called Arbello, who quit on the spot and went home the minute he'd got his hands on his money. The other guys were never paid, though everyone had contracts. The Union in the US wouldn't help us despite the contracts.

So that was the problem with Perez Prado. It was a great experience playing in his band, because thanks to Paul Webster, who was a big help to me, I got back my strength as a player and started hitting high notes -Fs and things - as well as running all over my horn, which was a great thing. I was sorry we'd had a problem with Perez Prado because musically I'd have liked to continue with him, but it seems he just didn't get along with musicians, and had his own way of handling the finances. You just couldn't live with those kind of circumstances.

I came back to New York and looked for a job. Paul and I had an opportunity to go to Paraguay where we were offered good salaries. In the end, he didn't want to do it, so we came back again to New York.

A small Latin band just starting out, hired me. They liked me a lot after I made a hit record with them. The band was led by Ricardo Ray and Bobby Cruz. After that I went back to Machito, who re-hired me now that I had some experience with Latin bands.

Machito's band went off on a tour to Japan and we played at a place called the Golden Alaska. There was a microphone on stage that led down to a speaker in the dressing room of the Japanese band that played opposite us. Their valet was learning to play saxophone, and he was a great player. He used to practise along with the sounds over the speaker.

They had an automatic stage there. When our band had finished, our stage would start to descend, and the Japanese band would come up right alongside on their stage.

During the time I was working with Latin bands, I had made

61

up my mind to go and live in Spain. But having met my wife in Argentina, and bringing her back to New York, that kind of messed up my plans to go to Spain. I did all right with Prado and those other Latin bands, but what I really knew how to do was play jazz. But I was still typecast as a lead trumpeter, and there were no jobs in jazz for lead trumpeters. I was like an old rag cast aside, no good any more. So I had to work hard to see if I could work again playing jazz, once I'd decided to live in New York again.

There was a time, while I was still married to my second wife, when I nearly went to live in France. This would have been shortly after the time I left Cab.

Through all the Spanish and Latin musicians I knew, I'd met this Cuban fellow who was a trombone player. He had a day job as a barber, and he was one hell of a barber. He had all the Spanish cats in New York going to his barber shop. One day he decided, he and his wife, that is, to move to Paris. So they shut up the barber shop and set off for France. She was a milliner, I understand, and she did very well there, setting herself up in business in Paris, because she was a real expert. And he organized a band.

So he wrote and told me all about it. He invited me to come and join his band, and because he was a great man, and he liked me, I said I'd come. So I did.

I packed up everything, and he had me get some big books for him to put the music in for each instrument. I had about ten of these big box files that you use to store the parts for each instrument and somehow I fitted them in with all the other things I was taking to Paris. I had made up my mind: "I'm going over there, and if I like it I'm going to stay."

So I got on the boat. It was almost the last time I saw my second wife, because we'd decided to split anyway. I was crossing on the SS United States. About half way over there was some war scare on the boat. You're half way across the Atlantic and suddenly there's a scare on about things not going right in Europe. Every day there were different radio messages: one day things look better; the next day things look really bad; the next day everything has changed again.

So the people on the boat warned us things were going on. When we got to Le Havre, they gave us all instructions: "Those who want to return immediately to New York, stay on the boat! All those that want to get off do so at their own risk! Anyone who does get off should immediately get a flashlight, a torch, because there may possibly be blackouts at night."

Well the people were as scared as hell. And here am I over there, going all the way to a new life in Paris. I was one of them that got off, took a chance. I said to myself, "Maybe they'll straighten this business out and there won't be any war."

I got the train in Le Havre, and I went to Paris. I got off the train at night, and it was coal black - no lights in the city at all. I had the address of this Cuban fellow that sent for me to come and play in his band. But I couldn't find him. I couldn't even find anyone who knew anything about this man. So I made my way up to a little hotel in Montmartre. Every night it was blackout. And I was stuck there. I couldn't find nothing or nobody, so I decided I'd better get the hell out of there.

I had a little wooden trunk with me, a travelling wardrobe trunk. It had had to be carried up to the hotel. I left it there while I went down to the railroad station to see about getting away. There were people running, running all over the streets of Paris. All of them were getting out of town and all that stuff. I went to find out about a ticket, but there were no ticket sellers. Instead, people were running all through the railroad station, jumping on the trains without tickets. And the trains themselves were all packed, with people hanging off the back of the cars.

So I went hurrying back to the hotel. I went and got my trunk, and all by myself I pulled and tugged it all the way down from Montmartre to the Gare St. Lazare. I pulled it up the steps into the Station, and I finally set it down in the middle of the concourse. So now what am I going to do? There were no porters. There was nothing.

People were still running around like hell.

So what I did was I left the trunk exactly where it was, and I grabbed a place hanging on the back of a train going to Le Havre, until we stopped in a place called Rouen. That's in the middle, about halfway between Paris and Le Havre. I was as hungry as hell, so I got off to see if I could dash across the street to the bar to get a sandwich. The bar was absolutely packed with people, all of them with the same idea as me. It took the barman ages to serve me, and no sooner had I finally got a piece of bread and some ham when I heard the railroad train toot toot like they're going to pull out. And they did - but very slowly. I ran out of that bar with my piece of ham and bread, and I raced the train up the platform. Finally I caught it, and I hung on to the back there all the way to Le Havre.

I found a hotel in Le Havre. It was a sad, worn-out, old time hotel, but it was very cheap. I stayed the night there, and the next morning I went to find the consul. I told him I had to get back home, but I had no money, and this, that and the other. He was very nice to me, but his office was full of people, all crowded in. They all had the same story, more or less, screaming and hollering that they wanted to go home. A lot of them even had first class tickets. I had to tell the man I didn't even have a ticket, and what's more I didn't have any money either - certainly not enough to get home on.

Well, he seemed to like me. I went down there every morning and stayed in his office. Sometimes I was crowded in because there were so many people. He usually called me to come in to his office through the back door, he'd beckon me through the crowd to come, and I'd go round there. Finally, one day he said: "Look. Here's a note. Take this to pier number so-and-so at such-and-such a time, and get on this boat."

I think the boat was named Schodack. It was a freighter. But as he told me about it, I said: "I've got nothing." He looked at me, and then he gave me an IOU for me to sign that would cost me sixty-odd dollars to get on this freight boat.

So, the next morning I got ready to go there. I went downstairs early in my hotel to pay the bill, but shortly before I got down there the owner had been arrested, and I understand later he was shot. So there was nobody there to pay. There was no food either. The only food in the place was in an icebox in the kitchen. I found some sausages, some stale bread and an open bottle of wine. People were just going in there and helping themselves. That's how we ate, how I ate.

Eventually I got down there to the pier. I got on board and it took fourteen days to get back to New York. They had army cots all along the bottom of the boat, all in a line. I don't know how many people they actually had on board, it seemed they didn't take too many people. But those that were there ate upstairs with the crew. The food was out of sight. Really great. Potatoes and beef stews, things like that every day. Fresh bread. But we had to get up every morning and take a shower on the deck. They'd set up a big shower thing for us. We had to wash all our clothes, too, because the rules on that boat were that everybody had to keep themselves clean.

During that fourteen days, coming back to New York, there were submarines trailing the boat, and everyone was scared as hell. All this happened in September 1939, just at the start of the last war. That was an experience I had.

After I came back to New York, my second wife took me back into the apartment we had, but our marriage was already over. Anyhow, some years after I got back from France I received a telegram from the American Express people, telling me to come down and collect my trunk. After the war was over, this trunk of mine had been sent all the way back to New York, and the American Express people had known where to send it, because it had my name written all over it. I went down there, and it didn't cost me a dime when I picked it up and brought it back. That was the greatest thing that happened, because everything I had was in that trunk. When I quit France, I didn't even have a clean pair of socks. So although I was going to live in France, I was glad I got the hell out of there!

After that I've never wanted to go back to Europe to live. I changed my mind about that, not just because of the wartime experience, but because of the language. When you don't know the language where you're living, you have to take a lot of things and a lot of treatment you wouldn't normally take because you can't get on easily with the people of the country. I don't mean any big deal, just simple things like finding the best places to live, the best places to eat and so on. You have to take what you can find. Immediately before and just after the war some of the places to work weren't so good either.

It had been different with Sam Wooding. When I was over there with him there was so much going on you could pick your jobs and money was no object. But that was in the mid-20s. I found myself back in France looking for work around 1950, after the war. Things weren't so great in New York, so I came back over to France. I think it was on that trip I met up with Buck Clayton who was over at the same time, but many of the clubs were still closed and the country was still picking itself up after the war.

I know for certain it was in 1950 in Paris that I met up with Coleman Hawkins and Eartha Kitt. I played a concert with them, and then went on to do a record date with Eartha Kitt. I didn't get any money for the recording or the concert. The only thing the guy who organised it gave me was a huge bottle of Eau de Cologne. That's all I got. Then I picked up a one-nighter with James Moody, playing in a club called La Cigale. I played all night long, and I got $10 for that. But all in all things weren't working out quite like I'd expected them to be in Paris.

When Buck Clayton was there he had a problem with conflicting engagements. So he sent me out to a city called Nancy in his place. He had been advertised to play at this concert, so he sent me along with a French band. We all got on the train together and all the way from Paris to Nancy the other musicians worried the hell out of me.

It was "Do you know how to play this?" or "Do you know these changes to that?" By the time we got there I found out that they were playing New Orleans music, and I knew every one of those damn things from when I'd been in Chicago. The place was absolutely packed. Every seat was sold and there was standing room only. We went on stage and hit out on some New Orleans tune, and the band was swinging. I looked across and the manager of the place was standing in the wings biting his thumb because Buck wasn't there. But the place was so large that from the audience to the stage was far enough for them not to be able to tell if I was Buck Clayton or not. So they would holler: "Come on, Buck! Come on Buck!" And the band went right on swinging.

Everything was OK until the intermission. The curtain went down, and the applause was just marvellous. Things had only just died down when I heard the manager going out to make a speech. He was apologising to the people, saying that this was not Buck Clayton they'd been listening to, as he wasn't able to come, but Doc Cheatham who was here filling out. Well, naturally, the audience were kind of hurt. I could tell this from their reaction when we went back on. I guess if he hadn't said anything it would have gone unnoticed, and they'd have carried on having a great time. Obviously a few people there knew Buck, but most of them had never heard him before.

Nevertheless, in the end the second half picked up, and it was a fine experience. I got a few dollars as well. I sure was grateful to Buck, because when I set off there I didn't have one franc in my pocket and he really helped me out. I've always been very grateful to him for that. In the end, I came back to New York and worked some more with the Latin bands.

7
The Late Bloomer

After all my work with Latin American bands, it was actually George Wein that had most to do with getting me back into playing jazz. He was running a couple of clubs up in Boston in the early 1950s. They were called the Storyville and the Mahogany Hall. The Storyville was upstairs in the Copley Square Hotel, and the Mahogany Hall was downstairs in the basement.

Upstairs they had all kinds of jazz, he'd bring in Duke, Basie, Sarah Vaughan, all that kind of thing. Downstairs we just played dixieland. There was a good audience for it in Boston, and I think we may well have made more money down there than he was making upstairs. Vic Dickenson had the band, and Claude Hopkins was on piano, John Field on bass and Buzzy Drootin on drums. George couldn't find anybody who was available that knew that New Orleans music except me. It was the same music I'd learned in Chicago in the '20s, but there weren't too many people around New York or Boston that could play it, so that's why he hired me.

I spent overall maybe a couple of years in Boston, and during the time we were there my son was born.

People ask me if that was when I "rediscovered" jazz, while I was in Boston. But that wasn't it. I knew what they were playing, and I was the leader. The trumpet is the leader in a dixieland band, so it just came easy to me. It was just another job, but a very easy one.

Every Sunday, the two bands would get together. Whoever was upstairs at the Storyville and us. Generally that was the more modern type of jazz, and it was during this period I had the pleasure of playing alongside Charlie Parker, who'd been working upstairs. It was a lot of fun.

Once I'd got into the dixieland style of playing, I started to do more work. I was at Ryan's for a while with Danny Barker, maybe just a couple of weeks, and then back in Boston with the second band run by Wilbur De Paris. Wilbur used to lead his own band down in the clubs in New York, but he'd keep a second band going at the Savoy in Boston, and he'd come up on Saturdays, which was pay day, collect the money and pay the musicians.

In due course I ended up working with Wilbur's New York band. His brother Sidney had played trumpet for him for years, in fact on and off since we'd been together in Philadelphia in the 20s. But Sidney joined the Jehovah's Witnesses. They'd call on him and demand him to appear somewhere or other to do something for or about the church. And he'd just go, leaving Wilbur, who was working in Jimmy Ryan's at the time, without a trumpet player. So Wilbur hired me to come in there.

It was difficult coming into a band that had no music. They'd play all night long doing all kinds of different arrangements, but although all the arrangements were by Wilbur, none of them was written out. They were all "head" arrangements.

After he hired me, I realised I might be working with him quite a bit, so I brought along a little manuscript book. Every time we'd play a number, I'd write it down, everything about how we played it. I did that for his whole repertoire. I jotted down all the solos, when the drummer was to get a few bars, when Omer Simeon was supposed to pay his clarinet features, how many measures, and so on. So I could play some of the numbers I'd never heard before, Wilbur gave me his records, a whole pile of 78s. I took them home and I sat up after the job writing down all the arrangements, playing those discs on my machine over and over again until I had everything down. After about six months I reckoned I'd written out just about everything he ever did.

So I took the records back, along with the trumpet book I'd written out.

"Oh! This is beautiful!" he said. "I'd like you to make one for the whole band."

So I went home and did it. I made up a set of parts for the whole band. But when it was done I had to take him to the Union to get paid for it. He didn't want to pay me, and told me because I was playing in the band it was something I was supposed to do for no extra. But it wasn't. To try and explain what had been involved, I sat down with him, and I went through all the books, all the parts I had copied out so beautifully. (I was a good copyist.) I showed him how I'd put in every little cue, every detail of how he played his repertoire.

He looked at them and said: "They are great. This is wonderful. I just want to look them over." He looked them over, came back and said: "Gee! These are perfect. How did you do it?"

"I just sat up and did it."

He never said "How much do I owe you?" And for two months I didn't say anything more to him because I was working with him all the time.

Finally, one night he says: "Doc. What do I owe you for the copying?"

I said, "What do you want to give me, Wilbur? We're friends. I work for you."

He looked me up and down and he gave me $100.

I said, "Wilbur, this is awful."

He said, "Well, that's what I think it's worth."

That's what he thought. And I was mad at him. I went to the Musician's Union. I never did anything like that before in my whole life. I went in to the local and I explained what had happened. I took his records in there, and copies of some of the music. Of course, Wilbur kept the full set of parts I'd made. He wouldn't let those out of his sight. But I said to the people at the Union, "Look. I copied down everything on these 78s for Wilbur De Paris's Band. I wrote it all out, every note of it. And he gave me $100."

The guy said: "What?"

I said, "That's right. He gave me $100. What do you think I should get for it?"

They wouldn't give me a price. They said, "We're going to call him in to the Union."

So they set up a board meeting. Called him in. Called me in. But he never showed up, and he never paid me a nickel more.

I stayed with his band, though. I had to. I had no other job, so I just put up with it and stayed. After a while I wasn't angry with him. He just acted like it had never happened, forgot it. But I never saw that music again. Which is a pity, because if I ever had,

70

I was going to tear it up and take it home and burn it! He must've locked that music up in a safe somewhere because even when Garvin Bushell came in on clarinet, in place of Omer Simeon, from time to time, Wilbur never gave him the parts. He just had to manage as best he could, because he didn't know the book, but Wilbur wasn't going to bring those arrangements out while I was around.

One night I was playing with Wilbur at Ryan's, and I was doing some stuff with a plunger mute. A guy from the audience got very excited, then he jumped up and gave me a $20 bill. I stuck it in my pocket, and when we finished that set (we had a dressing room downstairs) we went down to the band room. I divided the money up with the rest of the guys, but not Wilbur. It came to about $4 apiece, something like that, and Sonny White said: "Man! You're going to get in trouble!"

I said, "What are you talking about?"

He said, "Wilbur's supposed to take all of those tips for himself,"

"What?" I said.

"Yes," said Sonny. "You can't keep that money."

But I did. And Wilbur never said one word to me. If anyone else in the band received a tip, they'd turn it over to him. He'd say, "This is my band, I'm paying you. So all of the tips belong to me."

That was his way. The way he ran the band. But he never said one word to me about the $20, or any other tips that I split with the others in the band, because he knew I'd quit. And I was important to him in the band, bacause if Sidney cut out, who else was going to lead them through all those arrangements? I knew them off by heart after writing them all out. So he never said one word about it.

It was great playing alongside Omer Simeon. We played pretty much the same stuff every night, except for solos of course, but Omer helped me a lot when I was getting to know the book. When I was writing out the arrangements he helped me a lot, too. He'd help me if I didn't get all of the details jotted down during our live sessions, because it was quite difficult playing one number and going to the next, but all the while scribbling down the bones of the arrangements for the stuff the band hadn't recorded. He really helped me with that, putting in a lot of the finer points.

But I'd been jotting down stuff I played or listened to since the 20s. I wrote out some of the things Louis played that I heard. I just had the talent for it, I guess. But I remembered a lot of what I heard in Chicago because I had it written down.

When I was teaching during the '40s, around the time I had my job in the Post Office, I had the idea to write out a book of exercises for beginners. I was trying to do something a little different, that would help learners with their ear training. I wrote out some choruses on different tunes, based on familiar chord sequences, and the first thing learners have to do is to identify the melody, then to work out for themselves how to play an ad-lib chorus over the same chords.

It seemed to work pretty well with my students, so I mailed it off to a publisher in England, and they accepted it. *Ad-Lib Chord Reading* by Adolphus (Doc) Cheatham was published by Feldman's of 64 Dean Street, just a few doors away from the Pizza Express where I was to play many times in the '80s. That was the only thing I ever had published, but it was very satisfying. I didn't earn a fortune from it in royalties, but it sold quite well for a time.

I stayed with Wilbur for quite a few years. He never knew when Sidney was going to be absent, so I'd be standing by for the telephone to ring from the club, and Wilbur to call me to run down there right away. Sidney wouldn't fly in a plane either, so that's how I came to make tours to Africa and to France with the band, because Sidney wouldn't travel. I did some recordings alongside Sidney, where he plays tuba as well as trumpet, and on others we do some two trumpet things together. I guess overall if Sidney could make it he did, and if he couldn't they'd call. That's the way it happened with those brothers. But, you know, Wilbur never did lose that tightness over money. Apparently he died after trying to tamper with the electric meter in his house. He ran out in the street and dropped dead, electrocuted.

Once I'd got back into playing, and begun to make a reputation again, especially for playing the older New Orleans style of jazz, the phone would ring for other kinds of work as well. A fellow named Handy got together a session featuring a singer called Juanita Hall. It came together all of a sudden. The recording people called Claude Hopkins, and Claude called me, and Coleman Hawkins and Buster Bailey, and we just turned up. That kind of thing happens very quickly. You don't have time to think, you just turn up there and do the recordings.

In 1958 I went back to France on a tour with Sammy Price. I think J.C. Higginbotham and Eddie Barefield were with us on that occasion. We got to Europe and did a concert in France. Then we were to go to Amsterdam. While we were there, Pope Pius XII died, and the rest of the tour was cancelled. We hung around Amsterdam a little while, doing nothing, waiting to see if something could be done, at least so we could earn our transportation back to America. Fairly soon, we'd all run out of money. Our agent was very nice, and got together with Sam Price to find enough money to get us back to Paris. So we got back to Paris, and we hung around there on our way back to New York, hoping that something would turn up to keep us there, so we didn't have to go straight back only having played one job of the tour.

I was really broke. The only thing I ate every day was the continental breakfast in our hotel which was free. Then one morning Sammy came back to the hotel and he says to me, "Come on, let's go!"

I said: "Where the hell are we going?"

"We're going to make some records."

So Sam and I went off together. The rest of the guys didn't know about it. By then, one or two of them had managed to get their fares together and go back, although some of them were still around the hotel. Sam and I went down town to a little recording studio, where we made an album for the Club Français Du Disque. It ws a little double album of George Gershwin tunes and we did it with just piano and trumpet - no drums or anything. The album came out wonderfully well.

When we'd finished recording, Sam went into the office and talked to the girl, and he came back with a pocket full of francs. I never saw so many francs in all my life. He gave me my share (I forget how much it was) and I went straight out of there and straight into the nearest restaurant and ordered up steak, and potatoes, and salad, and dessert. The whole works. After nearly starving, suddenly I was living like a king again.

Just after that, I went shopping. I went out to get some toilet water. I didn't know my way around Paris too well, but I came across what looked like a suitable store, and it had a perfume department on the second floor. I went upstairs and up to the sales counter.

The assistant looked straight at me and smiled. "Oh! Johnny Hodges!" she says, "How glad I am to see you! Look, I've been saving some samples for you." I had a pipe, and I had a cap on, because it was a cold day late in the year. I guess because Johnny smoked a pipe, and because of my hat, she thought I was Johnny. Anyhow, she beckoned me over to her desk, and gave me a great big bag full of perfume samples.

"I've been saving these for you, Johnny," she says. "Oh, I'm so happy to see you."

The place was full of people all looking at me, so I thanked her and turned round and made some kind of excuse to get out of there as quickly as I could before she realised I really wasn't Johnny Hodges.

As I flew down the stairs I could hear her calling: "Au revoir, Johnny! Au revoir!"

It was while I was in Europe with Sam Price the next time that I started singing. Sam came over quite regularly with six piece bands, like the one he had with Emmett Berry and Edmond Hall's brother, Herb. On this occasion, he had me, Ted Buckner and Gene Conners. The recording engineers wanted to balance the band, so they asked us to play something. We started to play a song, and I just sang the vocal when it came to the second chorus. They liked it, and I've been singing ever since.

I had to do a lot of things to correct my vocal technique because I really had no control to start with. I had to learn about voice control, vibrato, stuff like that, and it took me quite a long time to learn to do it how I wanted. But now, people seem to like it, and that's what counts.

By this time, my second career was getting under way. I guess I'm what you'd call a "late bloomer", but I'd finally shaken off the idea that I was just a lead trumpeter. People began to realise that I was a soloist in my own right. I started to get plenty of work, and I travelled quite a lot, not just in the US, but coming to Europe more often.

I came to London in the '60s with a package called "Top Brass". It was put together by an agency in England, who booked the group. They wanted me, Benny Morton, Clark Terry and Bob Brookmeyer to come over, with a rhythm section. I'd worked a few times before with Benny Morton, but only one nighters and odd dates, so it was nice to have the chance to work together for longer, as I got to know him really well.

The whole package was very successful. I sat in on a couple of the concerts with Maynard Ferguson's big band, just for kicks, but our own band was fun to play in as well. We did mostly one-nighters all across the UK and up into Scotland, staying in little places on the way. We ended up in the Albert Hall, I think - a wonderful gig.

Some time after I got back, I was working in the International Restaurant in New York with a little Latin Trio, when Benny Goodman's brother came in. It was a Jewish place, a nice restaurant and good floor shows, often imported from Las Vegas. Benny's brother obviously liked what he heard, because he spoke to Benny about using me, and that's how I came to work with Benny in the '60s.

I made a rehearsal, Benny auditioned me, and I passed. I was with him I guess for about a year. He had quite severe back problems, so we never went out on the road for long. I played mainly in his sextet. He wanted me to go in the full big band, when he got a tour to Belgium, but he was very tight with the money and it wasn't worthwhile to go over there and work hard in the World's Fair for what he was prepared to pay. After he'd been turned down by some of his regular band, like me, he started phoning around. He called Harry James.

"What does it pay?" Asked Harry.

"I'll pay you the same rates I did when you were in the band," said Benny.

Harry hung up on him.

I don't know who he took in the end. Later I went to Belgium with him with the sextet, but that was a different deal from the big band.

Many musicians had problems with Benny, but my time with him was great, and he treated me like a brother the whole time. He held daily rehearsals, and he loved that aspect of the band.

Once we were working in Las Vegas, playing side by side. It was difficult for me to see him, but he kept jumping from one tune to another when he felt like it, without telling me or anyone. He called me to his room.

"Doc, you must look at my left eye, all the time when we're on stage."

"Benny, I can't see your left eye from where I stand!"

With that he burst out laughing and we had no more trouble. I was generally so quiet I never said much to him. People told me you never knew how he'd react.

One morning on the road he came out of his hotel and saw me sitting across the street. He came over and said: "Doc, does anything ever bother you?"

"Only if you don't pay me!" I said.

Another time I was with Benny in Fort Lauderdale. During rehearsal, he asked us all if we'd found places to live while we were there. All the men said yes, except me. He then asked me where I was staying, as at that time the hotel where most of the rest of them were living would not admit me.

I stood up and told him, "I'm staying with Miss Car."

"Who's that?" he asked me.

"Miss Box Car," I said.

Benny laughed and found a nice place for me to stay.

So I never had any trouble working with Benny Goodman.

I was very happy once when Duke Ellington had his sister call me up and ask me to join the band. That was one of the greatest offers I have ever had in my life, to join Duke's band. And this was a permanent job, I could have stayed as long as I wanted to. He was going to Japan, and he wanted me to go.

When she called I was lying in bed. I'd just come out of hospital with a hernia repair, and the doctors had told me not to play for between six and eight weeks. So I couldn't accept the job.

Before he died, I read an article about Duke, which I've kept to this day, where he said the only thing he was sorry about was he didn't get a chance to record with Doc Cheatham. Man, that struck me so. I feel so wonderful he thought that much of me. He didn't have to say that, after all he was Duke Ellington and he'd made all those other wonderful records.

One of the greatest thrills I had as a musician was just around that time, in the mid-1960s. I went over to the East Side to a night club where Red Allen was playing. I had heard Red at various times, and I knew him quite well. But on this occasion I went and sat at a table near the band and stayed there all night. He did three or four shows, and I stayed through them all. I learned more about Red Allen than I ever knew. I learned what a great showman he was, and what a great entertainer. You have to sit and listen to a guy all night to understand what makes a musician a great star. He was out of sight, Red Allen, and from him I learned a lot of the things I needed to do to improve my own playing.

I had a similar experience in Detroit, listening to Dizzy Gillespie and his big band. I sat at the side of the stage after my set had finshed, and watched Dizzy play the final set of the concert. I sat there in the wings and looked and listened. He was a great entertainer, and he had the people in the palm of his hand. Despite his reputation, Miles Davis was the same, he could control an audience, have them eating out of his hand. I sat through two of his performances and he knew exactly what to do. It was the same tradition of great entertainers that Cab, and Louis and Dizzy and Red Allen were all part of. Being a great entertainer is what it's all about.

8
Sweet Basil And World Travel

In the late 1970s the Roosevelt Hotel here in New York renovated its ground floor restaurant and renamed it the Crawdaddy. They decided they wanted to have some jazz, and the booking agent called me. They decided to put in a trio, so as well as me there was a pianist and a drummer, and our three pieces played right there in the dining room.

We only went in there for a weekend, for the hotel management to see what we sounded like, and ended up staying four or five years. Eventually the hotel was sold to some people from India or Pakistan, I forget which, and they didn't want any music at all, so they closed it down. But we were lucky, because we went straight to Sweet Basil in the Village. They heard about how good we sounded, and we started there playing the Sunday brunch, adding an extra instrument, the bass, and making it a quartet. Again we went in there for one weekend, on trial, and I've been there ever since, over fifteen years now.

It had taken me a long while to feel I was where I wanted to be again playing jazz. George Wein, Wilbur De Paris and Red Balaban (who had a band in the Village) all helped to get me back to playing jazz. Back in the 1950s, before I worked for George Wein, I was in Boston, playing in a little beer joint in New London, trying to get my jazz chops working again. I was listening to Roy Eldridge, Charlie Shavers, Buck Clayton, people like that, and I'd begun to think I should just give up. Then someone said, "Keep pushing. Get all that lead trumpet crap out of your mind. You're no longer a lead trumpet player, so get it out of your head!"

That was a problem I had, and until that moment I couldn't think straight. I stayed up in New London a long while playing trumpet. I knew there was something missing, and I felt the same way when I was working with Red Balaban. I stuck it out, and I knew all the dixieland tunes, but my soul wasn't in it.

The real turning point for me was when George Wein sent me to Nice in France. I did my best, but I was thrown in the company of Clark Terry, Bobby Hackett and all those guys. I felt so ashamed of myself, but something kept pushing me to keep going. I knew how bad I sounded because I heard some sets from the festival on the radio. I wasn't a fool, and I didn't go round thinking I was something big.

But I stuck with George Wein, and he was very nice and sent me back again and again. Each time I went on one of his tours I felt myself getting better and better. I lost a lot of friends. A lot of people turned their backs on me during my recovery, but I didn't give a damn. I stuck it out and slowly but surely started to get somewhere.

Then George sent me to Russia with a big band. I went over there with five trumpet players. I felt bad, but I was working on it, and during the trip I felt I was constantly getting better, concentrating more and learning the things I didn't know. I tried to improve my style, because as a soloist, I had no real style at all. Having never had a teacher, I had to learn by listening to other musicians. For example, I went on a jazz cruise with Dizzy Gillespie, Ruby Braff, Clark Terry and Sweets Edison. I sat back and listened to those guys. I didn't want to copy from anyone, I just wanted to listen and improve myself my way.

Of course I could remember a lot of what I'd heard during my career. Louis, of course, and Tommy Ladnier and Freddie Keppard had all been influences on my playing. Another influence was a guy named Canaro who I met in Europe with Sam Wooding. He came from Argentina and played in the Great Canaro Brothers Tango Band. He played on the bandstand opposite Sam in Biarritz, and I made friends with him, and he showed me things I'd never heard of. His own playing was outta sight, and for some sets we would swap trumpet players, and he and I would alternate between the bands.

In the 1960s and 1970s, as my playing was improving, I worked with the Duke Ellington alumni, from whom I learned a lot, and I've also played with Count Basie's alumni group. I still play from time to time with society bands here in New York. I learn a lot by sitting at home studying. I get my horn out and practice, and learn some new melodies and see what I can do with

79

them. For my recent Columbia album, "The 87 Years of Doc Cheatham" I learned and recorded Monk's "Round Midnight" for the first time in my career.

I've managed to avoid major health problems, although since my 80th birthday I've been waiting around for things to go wrong, and there seems to be an endless stream of minor problems. If it's not one thing it's another: ear infection, eye infection, tests for melanoma, hammertoe operations, prostate checkups, gall bladder checkups, dentistry. I have to get my teeth checked over regularly, and I'm starting to lose some pressure in my playing, with the gaps in my teeth. I'm also on a diet now. Being my age, I've had to cut out all fat, greasy or fried foods, no gravy, no salt, no sugar. Once in a while I can eat a piece of lean beef, an egg, shrimps, or slip in a piece of fried catfish with saffron. But I'm watching my diet and I have to cut out all those delicious pies and things when I get to Europe. In France or Austria I see all those delicious delicacies, and have to turn my back on them. I eat things nowadays that I can't stand, but I know I have to, or face the consequences.

Even so, my playing has been getting better as I go through my eighties. I had a lot of fun in the Calloway band reunions. I particularly enjoyed a couple of concerts with Cab at Carnegie Hall. I didn't play in Cab's band, but Milt Hinton, Eddie Barefield and Panama Francis came on with me as alumni. Only a year or two before Cab's death, he and I rode together on the top lounge of a 747 on our way to Norway, and we had a ball talking about old times.

Since George Wein helped me get back on my feet, musically, I have really managed to travel the world. I was in Japan with one of Machito's last bands, playing Afro-Cuban music for three or four weeks. I got a chance to hear some other bands in Japan, and made some recordings there, with a Japanese band called the Blue Notes. I really enjoyed Japan, but there was a language problem. I simply couldn't learn any Japanese.

I managed two or three simple things like "goodbye", "good morning" and "thank you", but anything else was very difficult.

I still recall a smattering of the languages in all the places I went to with Sam Wooding, and I feel better when I can greet a person, read a menu and ask simple questions. I have enough German to get by, and after all that time with Latin bands, I have learned quite a bit of Spanish. I've already said how knowing the language is important if you're going to live in a foreign country, but I also think it makes a big difference if you are just visiting.

I went to a jazz club in Vienna a few years ago. I'd been there over sixty years earlier with Sam Wooding, when we played up at the Pinehouse Hotel at Semmering in the Alps. When I went back to Vienna, some of the local people took me up to Semmering again. It looks the same, but if anything even more beautiful.

The people in Vienna treated me very well. They'd put out lots of publicity about how I'd been there sixty years ago with Sam at the Moulin Rouge, and the place was packed every night. A lot of elderly people came to hear this old trumpeter in his 80s who'd been there so long ago; professors, teachers, musicians, they all came to hear what it was all about.

One night I greeted the audience in the only German I knew, and they all applauded me. I had such a wonderful time there I went back again. Now I know my way around the modern city and can ask questions if I want to know something. I can go into the stores, or into restaurants to order food. It makes a big difference. I'm not so good at French. That's my worst language, but even there I can get around without being a dummy. I like to walk, still, where it's possible, and to bring back souvenirs and things from all my travels.

Of course I travel quite a bit in the US, and I still look out for souvenirs. One of the things I most enjoyed in this country was playing concerts in Detroit with the New McKinney's Cotton Pickers. I'm not the only musician still living from the original band, but there aren't too many of us left, even though they chopped and changed musicians a lot during the later years. I was inducted into the Hall Of Fame in Detroit, which was wonderful, and on my first visit up there I played two concerts.

In my playing days I wasn't ever a vocalist with the band, just playing lead. But now, since I've been at Sweet Basil, playing what I want, and doing my own stuff, I've learned a lot of vocals on old Cotton Pickers tunes. I've been singing "I Want A Little Girl" for a long time, but I've also learned "OK Baby", and "Cherry" and "Travelin'". So at the first concert in Detroit they put me out in front of the band, right on the edge of the stage. They asked me before the concert what I knew, and so I made a schedule of the five or six vocals that I would sing. When I got there, they'd made up a list for me, with all the lyrics and the keys of the arrangements, because at Sweet Basil I play in whatever key I feel like, but the old arrangements were in particular keys for the big band. I played solos on most of the pieces in the concert, and sang my vocals. I really liked that, because that's how you should be treated, to make you comfortable so you know exactly what you're doing.

I have the same thing when I come to England to play with the big band called Harlem. We do a Cotton Club show, which I have played many times with Benny Waters as the other featured guest, playing tenor and alto, and just like with the New Cotton Pickers, I sit out in front, not in the section, and play solos. We last did the show at the Barbican Hall in London.

At this stage of the game I enjoy playing with different groups in Europe and elsewhere whom I don't regularly work with. They seem to have more respect for you than when you go out with more familiar groups of musicians you know, although I did have a great time some years ago playing concerts in New York and France with Lionel Hampton's big band.

I'd rather work with a big band like Lionel's than some of the other large orchestras I've played with in the more recent past. There was a fashion about the time I was getting back into jazz for brass sections to cut out their vibrato entirely, and you'd see the parts all marked with "N.V." for "No Vibrato". I could never understand why they did that, bacause although it's easy to do, it made the tone of a band sound thin.

Then they'd introduce what I call "backward beat". This was something the white big bands got into, where they started playing behind the beat instead of exactly on the beat. I could never do that, in fact I thought it was one of the worst things ever to happen in jazz. You'd hear a guy playing a solo, and the rhythm and the section are on the beat, and he's playing way behind it. I was glad when that fashion got left behind, but I still hear a few guys around that can't do anything but that. They're mostly white players, because black players play smack on the beat the whole time. We don't know any other way of playing.

Session musicians would mark all kinds of things on their sheet music. As well as "N.V.", they might draw a pair of eyeglasses on a certain part of the arrangement. That means "be careful", because something is going to happen, like changing from four-four to three-four time.

When I'd play in bands backing singers, they'd bring with them a great pile of stock arrangements, and hand them out to all the guys in the band. They had these songs played for them on tours, and they would use the same music year in, year out. Everywhere they'd go, the same old parts would come out, and perhaps the M.D. would change some sections, so the band would mark it up on the parts: "Now we're going to jump from letter A straight to C, and then when we get to the end we play the tag and go right back to A".

Not all musicians would use pencil, that could be erased. They'd take out pens and scratch in the changes, and before long there'd be wholesale confusion in the ranks as the musicians got all screwed up with the different cuts marked on the music. I played once for Diahann Carroll somewhere downtown, playing lead trumpet in the section. My heart fell when I saw the parts, with all the bars written all over and some of the notes scratched out completely. Omit this, omit that, repeat this, repeat that. I did a lousy job because I couldn't understand it. I guess everybody in the band put me down, because I was supposed to be a lead trumpet, and I was supposed to be able to read anything, but if everything's covered in scratched out markings you can't make head nor tail of it. Perhaps it hurt my reputation for a while, but I didn't give a damn. I told the M.D. I wasn't going to play better until he copied the damn parts. I wasn't going to get bawled out on the stand for coming in in the wrong place or not knowing the cuts.

Whenever this happens now, I say to whoever, the singer or

the leader, "Look, I can't play this because I don't know where to start. So would you look on my sheet and explain where I'm supposed to come in?" Nine times out of ten they can't tell you. They figure you should just know it and look at you with a smirk on their faces. So now, playing with my quartet at Sweet Basil, I really don't have to worry about reading music any more, and that suits me just fine.

When I started at Sweet Basil the quartet was with Chuck Folds on piano, Jackie Williams, drums, and Al Hall on bass. Then Al died, and Bucky Calabrese joined. He was a friend of Al's and has been with the quartet for many years now, although he's been sick recently. I don't travel too much with the quartet. When I do go abroad it's usually on my own, playing with local musicians, or with groups of other stars of the swing era.

Sometimes I get to play with other musicians I would not normally have the chance to play with. Like for instance at Nice, on my second trip there, I played with the Preservation Hall Band out of New Orleans. I played a couple of times with them on the Festival and also travelled to Nimes to play a concert. They didn't speak to me much, and although I was glad to meet and work with other musicians of my own age, I didn't find them particularly friendly. They seemed to be critical of me standing up to take solos.

I had a great time playing with the French band led by Maxim Saury, and also joining in every night at the jam sessions at the Meridian Hotel, where I had the pleasure of playing alongside Lockjaw Davis. Lockjaw and a group of other tenor players tore up the festival that year with a "battle of the tenors". I remember him fighting it out with Illinois Jacquet, Budd Johnson, and Eddie Barefield.

Cootie Williams was there that year, and we spent a lot of time with one another because our two groups travelled together, and we played quite a lot. That year I was with Sir Charles Thompson, George Duvivier and Vic Dickenson, and after Nice was over, they sent us together with Panama Francis and Eddie Barefield to San Sebastian in Spain. We played a festival there for two days, and then went to a town called Sitges, which is beautiful - about 45 minutes out of Barcelona. In Barcelona we made records with Carrie Smith, which I think were her first.

When I got back, I payed a concert in a park in the Bronx. What a contrast! We had a beautiful band playing, but the people were sitting way out in the street with their backs turned to the music, just like they'd sit out any other hot night, band or no band. It broke me up, after coming from France and Spain where people crowd all round you to hear every note you're playing, to be back in a country where nobody gives a damn whether you're playing or not. It makes me wonder, the people in our own cities don't want to hear our music, but in foreign countries it's all they want to hear. I can't figure it out.

The fans in Europe know more about the musicians than we know ourselves. They come up to you and tell you where you were born, who you played with, and as often as not, they bring along records you've made, pictures and write-ups, and you autograph them all day long. Even kids come up and say: "Are you Doc Cheatham who played with so-and-so?" That goes on everywhere in Europe and Japan, they wine you and dine you, bow to you and respect you.

It hurts sometimes to get off the plane back in New York, and nobody cares whether you play saxophone or telephone. It brings you down, but there's still no place like home. We just have to go to Europe and play better when we get there because we know we're being listened to carefully!

One question that comes up again and again when I travel, in interviews and in write-ups is about my hairdo. They all ask why I comb my hair forward, and I have had to explain it many times. I used to be troubled with cysts on the back of my neck, and no doctor could understand why. Then when I was in Japan, I went to a barbershop, and the woman who was doing my hair asked me to comb it all forward. She told me I had an allergy due to my hair on my neck at the back, and from that day on, I've combed it forward and have never been troubled again by cysts.

There is one place in the USA where what I've said about the indifference of American audiences is not true. That's New Orleans. In the last few years they've invited me down there several times, and I'm happy to know that the people there are very fond of me. In the last couple of years I've been running down there pretty often, and I've made a couple of albums in New Orleans and played concerts with Butch Thompson as well as appearing on the Festival. This is like a new career for me, and I've made friends with many of the musicians there like the drummer Ernie Elly (who I played with in Europe) and the young clarinettist Brian O'Connell, who just gets better all the time and plays on my latest album. So many of the young boys there are getting just a little too modern in their playing. Many, many tourists go there, and they find it disappointing if what they hear is getting too far away from the jazz of the past. Louis Armstrong died too soon, I think that's the reason.

I'm always keen to hear new musicians getting started. One player who's no baby now, but I've known practically since he started is little Warren Vaché. He's a white trumpeter, but he can scare the hell out of you. I'm so proud of him, and I've been following the course of his career. He has interest and creativity in his playing, and I think he's been running just a little ahead of most other players for a year or two now. But there's a cycle in these things, and as Warren gets older there'll be some new kids along to scare him and give him a hard time. That's the way it goes.

One of the kids who's probably going to be the greatest jazz player of our times is the young trumpet player Nicholas Payton, from New Orleans. He first sat in with me at Sweet Basil when he was just 20 years old, and he's making great strides in his playing. I feel that playing alongside him, and other trumpeters like Jon Faddis, Wynton Marsalis and my old buddy Clark Terry, I'm still learning. In the last year I've played on a couple of concerts at Carnegie Hall alongside Nicholas and Jon Faddis, and George Wein still keeps me busy on his JVC Festival.

My travels to Europe are getting fewer now I'm in my ninetieth year. No-one cares to take the chance: what with my arthritis and stiff legs and knees I must be starting to look like a cripple! But my chops are as good as ever, and I think my jazz has improved so much.

Even so, as I write this I'm planning to go to Scotland and to Sweden this summer, if all goes according to plan. And in the meantime, I'm at Sweet Basil, where people from all over the world come and pack the place out every Sunday brunch.

Although I used to teach jazz and trumpet, when young players come up to me at the club and ask for instructions concerning how to pay jazz, I'm less sure than ever. What can I tell them? It's been 89 years and I can't understand it myself?

I just hope the chops hold out a little longer.

Recording Chronology

by Howard Rye

Scope: This discography covers Doc Cheatham's jazz recordings, excluding those with the Cab Calloway Orchestra (see note after session of 8 September 1931). For reasons of space, only original issues are included. These are 10" 78 r.p.m. issues up to the session of 31 January 1950, unless shown in italics, which indicates an LP (or a CD where so marked). All subsequent issues listed are 12" LPs, unless noted as 45 SP, EP, or CD. Doc Cheatham has also made recordings with Latin-American ensembles and has appeared with studio groups accompanying popular singers; these recordings are omitted here.

Countries of origin: All records listed are of United States origin unless coded after the label name, as follows:

(Ca)	Canadian		(G)	German
(Da)	Danish		(J)	Japanese
(Du)	Dutch		(Sd)	Swedish
(E)	British		(Ss)	Swiss
(F)	French			

Abbreviations (Instruments, etc.):

a	arranger		g	guitar
ah	alto horn		h	harmonica
as	alto saxophone		ldr	leader
b	bass		p	piano
bar	baritone saxophone		o	organ
bb	brass bass (tuba or sousaphone)		perc	percussion
bj	banjo		sb	double bass
c	cornet		ss	soprano saxophone
cl	clarinet		t	trumpet
d	drums		tb	trombone
ep	electric piano		ts	tenor saxophone
euph	euphonium		tu	tuba
f	flute		v	vocal
fh	flugelhorn		vb	vibraphone

Abbreviations (Other)

CD	Compact Disc	EP	Extended Play (45 r.p.m. disc)
CTJC	Connecticut Traditional Jazz Club	SP	Standard Play

Acknowledgements: For assistance in compiling this discography thanks are due to Gordon Bailey, Alan Bates, Derek Coller, Terry & Jan Dash, Barry Fleming, Gosta Hagglof, John Holley, John Norris, Norbert Ruecker, Alyn Shipton, Val Wilmer and, of course, Doc Cheatham himself.

Bibliography:
The following works have been consulted:
Walter Bruynincx, *70 Years Of Recorded Jazz: 1917-1987*, Mechelen, Belgium, 1987- (in progress).
Walter Bruynincx, *Modern Discography, Modern Jazz: Be-Bop, Hard Bop, West Coast* (6 vols), Mechelen, Belgium, 1984-1987.
Walter Bruynincx, *Progressive Discography, Progressive Jazz: Free, Third-Stream, Fusion* (5 vols), Mechelen, Belgium, 1984-1989.
Walter Bruynincx, *Swing Discography, Swing//1920-1985, Swing/Dance Bands & Combos* (12 vols), Mechelen, Belgium, 1986-1990.
Walter Bruynincx, *Traditional Discography, Traditional Jazz//1897-1985, Origins/New Orleans/ Dixieland/Chicago Styles* (6 vols), Mechelen, Belgium, 1987-1990.
Walter Bruynincx, *Vocalists Discography, The Vocalists 1917-1986, Singers & Crooners*, Mechelen, Belgium, 1989-1990.
O. Flückiger, *Lionel Hampton, Selected Discography 1966-1978*, First Revised Edition, Reinach, Switzerland, 1980.
Charles Fox, Peter Gammond, Alun Morgan, *Jazz On Record, A Critical Guide*, London, 1960.
Ralph Laing & Chris Sheridan, *Jazz Records, The Specialist Labels* (2 vols), Copenhagen, Denmark, 1981.
Albert McCarthy, 'Swing Era Recordings', *Mainstream*, No. 1 (Summer 1974), 4-6.
Alfredo Papo, *El Jazz A Catalunya*, Barcelona, Spain, 1985.
Vincent Pelote, *The Complete Commodore Jazz Recordings, A Discography*, Stamford, CT, 1990.

Erik Raben (ed.), *Jazz Records 1942-80, A Discography*, Copenhagen, Denmark, 1989- (in progress).

Michel Ruppli, *Atlantic Records, A Discography, Volume 1*, Westport, CT, & London, 1979.

Michel Ruppli, *Discographies, Vol. 1, Swing*, Paris, 1989.

Brian Rust, *Jazz Records 1897-1942*, 5th Revised and Enlarged Edition, Chigwell, Essex, England, n.d [1984].

Howard Rye, 'Discography' in Art Hodes and Chadwick Hansen, *Hot Man, The Life Of Art Hodes*, Champaign, IL, & Oxford, England, 1992.

Bob Weir, *Buck Clayton Discography*, Chigwell, Essex, England, 1989.

Bob Weir, 'Discography' in Sammy Price, *What Do They Want? A Jazz Autobiography*, Oxford, England,1989, 85-150.

Various editions of the *Bielefelder Katalog Jazz* (ed. Manfred Scheffner), and of *Bulletin du Hcf* and *Collectors Items* magazines.

MA RAINEY

Ma Rainey, v; acc. Her Georgia Band: Homer Hobson, c; Albert Wynn, tb; Tom Brown, cl/as; Doc Cheatham, ss; unknown, musical saw; Lil Henderson, p; Rip Bassett, bj; Ben Thigpen, d.

Chicago.		c. June 1926
2627-1	Down In The Basement	Paramount 12395
2628-1	Sissy Blues	Paramount 12384
2629-1	Broken Soul Blues	Paramount 12384

Some discographies quote a different personnel for this session based on a report in the *Chicago Defender* of 3 July 1926 giving the personnel of Ma Rainey's touring band. However, Doc Cheatham himself recalls this as his first recording session and his only recorded performances on saxophone. He also recalls recording with Tiny Parham, but the results, if issued, have not been reliably identified.

MAESTRO SAM WOODING Y SUS CHOCOLATE KIDDIES

Bobby Martin, t/v-1; Doc Cheatham, Tommy Ladnier, t; Al Wynn, Billy Burns, tb; Willie Lewis, cl/as/bar/v-2; Jerry Blake, cl/as/v-3; Gene Sedric, cl/ts; Freddy Johnson, p/v-4; John Mitchell, bj; Sumner Leslie 'King' Edwards, bb; Ted Fields, d/v-5; Sam Wooding, ldr.

Barcelona, Spain.		early July 1929
76517-2	I Can't Give You Anything But Love -5	Parlophon 25423
76518-2	Bull Foot Stomp -1, 4	Parlophon 25424
76519-2	Carrie -2, 3, 4, 5	Parlophon 25420
76520-2	Tiger Rag -4	Parlophon 25420
76521- -	Blake's Blues -1, 2, 3,	*Harlequin(E)* HQ2026
76521-2	Sweet Back Blues -1, 2, 3	Parlophon 25421
76522-2	Indian Love -5	Parlophon 25424
76523-2	Ready For The River -3	Parlophon 25422
76524-2	Mammy's Prayer -2	Parlophon 25422
76525-2	My Pal Called Sal -2	Parlophon 25421
76526-2	Krazy Kat	Parlophon 25423

Carrie was arranged by Doc Cheatham.

It has recently been stated on the basis of known recording dates of adjacent matrices that this session took place on 9/10 April 1929, but contemporary catalogues state that they were recorded "durante su estancia en Barcelona (Julio 1929)" and other research has established that the band actually appeared in Barcelona from 6-30 June, so that a recording date immediately after this seems indicated.

SAM WOODING AND HIS ORCHESTRA
Bobby Martin, t/v-1; Doc Cheatham, Harry Cooper, t; Al Wynn, Billy Burns, tb; Willie Lewis, cl/as/bar/v-2; Jerry Blake, cl/as/v-3; Gene Sedric, cl/ts; Freddy Johnson, p/v-4; John Mitchell, bj; Sumner Leslie 'King' Edwards, bb; Ted Fields, d/v-5; Sam Wooding, ldr.

Paris, France		c. 24 October 1929
300480-1	Smiling Irish Eyes -2, 3, 5	Pathé X8697
300481-1	Hallelujah! -2, 3, 5	Pathé X8696
300482-1	Downcast Blues -2, 3	Pathé X8684
300483-1	Weary River -2	Pathé X8684
300483-2	Weary River -2	Pathé X8684

It is thought that Doc Cheatham is not present on subsequent Paris recordings by Sam Wooding and His Orchestra.

McKINNEY'S COTTON PICKERS
Rex Stewart, Joe Smith, Doc Cheatham, t; Ed Cuffee, Quentin Jackson, tb/v; Benny Carter, Jimmy Dudley, cl/as; Prince Robinson, ts; Todd Rhodes, p/vb; Dave Wilborn, g; Billy Taylor, bb/sb; Cuba Austin, d.

Camden, N.J.		8 September 1931
68300-1	Do You Believe In Love At Sight?	*RCA(F) 430.272*
68300-2	Do You Believe In Love At Sight?	Victor 22811
70495-1	Wrap Your Troubles In Dreams	Victor 22811
70495-2	Wrap Your Troubles In Dreams	*RCA(F) FXM1-7059*

Doc Cheatham recorded with Cab Calloway from the session of 7 June 1932 until at least the session of 2 November 1938. It is uncertain whether or not he was present at the sessions on 20 February and 28 March 1939. Full details of these sessions can be found in Brian A.L. Rust, *Jazz Records 1897-1942*.

Some sources list Doc Cheatham on trumpet with Benny Goodman Orchestra, 16 October 1934, but he himself says that he did not even meet Goodman until much later and is not on these recordings.

PUTNEY DANDRIDGE AND HIS ORCHESTRA
Doc Cheatham, t; Tom Mace, cl; Teddy Wilson, p; Allan Reuss, g; Ernest Hill, sb; Cozy Cole, d; Putney Dandridge, v.

	New York City.	10 December 1936
20384-1	I'm In A Dancing Mood	Vocalion 3399
20385-2	With Plenty Of Money And You	Vocalion 3399
20386-1	That Foolish Feeling	Vocalion 3409
20387-1	Gee! But You're Swell	Vocalion 3409

TEDDY WILSON AND HIS ORCHESTRA
Karl George, Harold Baker, Doc Cheatham, t; Floyd Brady, Jack Wiley, tb; Pete Clark, cl/as/bar; Rudy Powell, cl/as; Ben Webster, George Irish, ts; Teddy Wilson, p; Albert Casey, g; Al Hall, sb; J.C. Heard, d/v-1; Jean Eldridge, v-2; band v-3.

	New York City.	11 December 1939
25735-1	Wham (Re-Bop-Boom-Bam) -1, 3	Columbia 35354
25736-1	Sweet Lorraine -2	Columbia 35711
25737-1	Moon Ray	Columbia 35354
25738-1	Liza -2	Columbia 35711
25738-2	Liza -2	*Tax (Sd) M8018*

	New York City.	18 January 1940
26435-A	Crying My Soul Out For You -2	Columbia 35372
26436-A	In The Mood	Columbia 35372
26437-A	Cocoanut Grove	Columbia 35737
26438-A	71	Columbia 35737

BENNY CARTER AND HIS ORCHESTRA
Doc Cheatham, Lincoln Mills, Sidney DeParis, t; Vic Dickenson, Jimmy Archey, Joe Britton, tb; Benny Carter, Ernie Purce, Eddie Barefield, as; Fred Williams, Ernie Powell, ts; Sonny White, p; Herb Thomas, g; Charles Drayton, sb; Al Taylor, d; Maxine Sullivan, v-1

	New York City.	1 April 1941
063700-1	Midnight -1	Bluebird B11288
063701-1	My Favorite Blues	Bluebird B11288
063702-2	Lullaby To A Dream	*RCA(F) 741.073*
063703-1	What A Difference A Day Made -1	Bluebird B11197

EDDIE HEYWOOD AND HIS ORCHESTRA
Doc Cheatham, t; Vic Dickenson, tb; Lem Davis, as; Eddie Heywood, p; Al
Lucas, sb; Jack Parker, d.

New York City.		19 February 1944
A-4722-1	'T Ain't Me	Commodore C554
A-4722-TK1	'T Ain't Me #2	*Mosaic MR23-128*
A-4723-1	Indiana	Commodore C582
A-4723-2	Indiana #2	*Mosaic MR23-128*
A-4724-1	Blue Lou	Commodore C570
A-4724-2	Blue Lou #2	*Mosaic MR23-128*
A-4725-1	Carry Me Back To Old Virginny	Commodore C570
A-4724-2	Carry Me Back To Old Virginny #2	*Mosaic MR23-128*

New York City.		26 February 1944
A-4726-1	I Can't Believe That You're In Love With Me #3	*Mosaic MR23-128*
A-4726-2	I Can't Believe That You're In Love With Me	Commodore C577
A-4726-3	I Can't Believe That You're In Love With Me #2	*Mosaic MR23-128*
A-4727-1	Love Me Or Leave Me	Commodore C577
A-4728-1	Begin The Beguine	Commodore C1514
A-4728-TK1	Begin The Beguine #2	*Mosaic MR23-128*

New York City.		11 March 1944
A-4729-1	I Cover The Waterfront	Commodore C1514
A-4729-TK1	I Cover The Waterfront #2	*Mosaic MR23-128*
A-4734-1	Save Your Sorrow	Commodore C554
A-4734-2	Save Your Sorrow #2	*Mosaic MR23-128*
A-4735-1	Just You, Just Me #2	*Mosaic MR23-128*
A-4735-2	Just You, Just Me	Commodore C578
A-4736-1	'Deed I Do #2	*Mosaic MR23-128*
A-4736-2	'Deed I Do	Commodore C578
A-4737-1	Lover Man	Commodore C582
A-4737-TK1	Lover Man #2	*Mosaic MR23-128*

BILLIE HOLIDAY
Doc Cheatham, t; Vic Dickenson, tb; Lem Davis, as; Eddie Heywood, p;
Teddy Walters, g; John Simmons, sb; Big Sid Catlett, d; Billie Holiday, v.

New York City.		25 March 1944
A-4742-1/2	How Am I To Know #2	*Commodore XFL14428*
A-4742-3	How Am I To Know	Commodore C569
A-4742-TK1	How Am I To Know #3	*Mosaic MR20-134*
A-4743-1	My Old Flame	Commodore C585
A-4743-2	My Old Flame #2	*Commodore XFL14428*
A-4743-TK1	My Old Flame #3	*Mosaic MR20-134*
A-4744-1	I'll Get By	Commodore C553
A-4744-2	I'll Get By #2	*Commodore XFL14428*
A-4745-1	I Cover The Waterfront	Commodore C559
A-4745-	I Cover The Waterfront #2	*Commodore XFL14428*
A-4745-1	I Cover The Waterfront #3	*Mosaic MR20-134*

Doc Cheatham, t; Vic Dickenson, tb; Lem Davis, as; Eddie Heywood, p; John Simmons, sb; Big Sid Catlett, d; Billie Holiday, v.

New York City.		1 April 1944
A-4750-1	I'll Be Seeing You	Commodore C553
A-4750-2/3	I'll Be Seeing You #2	*Commodore XFL15351*
A-4750-TK1	I'll Be Seeing You #3	*Mosaic MR20-134*
A-4751-1	I'm Yours	Commodore C585
A-4751-2	I'm Yours #2	*Commodore XFL15351*
A-4751-TK1	I'm Yours #3	*Mosaic MR20-134*
A-4752-1	Embraceable You #2	*Commodore XFL15351*
A-4752-2	Embraceable You	Commodore C7520
A-4752-TK1	Embraceable You # 3	*Mosaic MR20-134*
A-4753-1	As Time Goes By	Commodore C7520
A-4753-2	As Time Goes By #2	*Commodore XFL15351*

UNA MAE CARLISLE
Doc Cheatham, t; Trummy Young, tb-1; Walter Thomas, ts; Una Mae
Carlisle, p/v; Cedric Hardwicke, sb; Wallace Bishop, d.

New York City.	20 October 1944
The Rest Of My Life -1	Joe Davis 7175
The Rest Of My Life (alt. take) -1	*Harlequin(E)*
	HQCD19 (CD)
That Glory Day	*Harlequin(E)*
	HQCD19 (CD)

SIR WALTER THOMAS AND HIS BAND
Doc Cheatham, t; Eddie Barefield, cl-1/as-2; Hilton Jefferson, cl-3/as-4;
Walter Thomas, Theodore McRae, ts; Buddy Safer, bar; Billy Taylor, p; Milt
Hinton, sb; Specs Powell, d.

New York City.	27 June 1945
Dee Tees -1, 3	Joe Davis 8131
Black Maria's Blues -1, 4	Joe Davis 8131
Back Talk -1	*Prestige PR 7584*
Bird Brain -1	*Prestige PR 7584*

DOC CHEATHAM/EARTHA KITT/ROSALIE KING
Doc Cheatham, t; Jacques Diéval, p; Emmanuel Soudieux, sb; Eartha Kitt,
v-1; Rosalie King, v-2.

Paris.	31 January 1950
OSW-644-1 Embraceable You	Swing 336
OSW-645-1 I Can't Give You Anything But Love -1	*Swing SW8410*
OSW-646-1 Solitude -1	*Swing SW8410*
OSW-647-1 Since I Fell For You -1	*Swing SW8410*
OSW-648-1 What Is This Thing Called Love -1	*Swing SW8410*
OSW-649-1 Blues -2	*Jazz Time(F)*
	789327-2 (CD)
OSW-650-1 Doc's Blues	Swing 336

VIC DICKENSON
Doc Cheatham, t; Vic Dickenson, tb; George Wein, p; John Field, sb; Buzzy
Drootin, d.

Boston, Mass.	1953
Jealous	Storyville EP110
	(EP)

Southie Is My Home Town	Storyville EP110 (EP)
Come Back Sweet Papa	Storyville EP110 (EP)
Muskrat Ramble	Storyville EP110 (EP)

PEE WEE RUSSSELL AND THE MAHOGANY HALL ALL STARS
Doc Cheatham, t; Vic Dickenson, tb; Pee Wee Russell, cl; George Wein, p; John Field, sb; Buzzy Drootin, d.

Storyville Club, Boston, Mass.	1953
We're In The Money	Storyville STLP308
Gabriel Found His Horn	Storyville STLP308
Sugar	Storyville STLP308
Missy	Storyville STLP308
Sweet And Slow	Storyville STLP308
Lulu's Back In Town	Storyville STLP308

MAHOGANY HALL ALL STARS
Doc Cheatham, t; Vic Dickenson, tb; Al Drootin, cl; George Wein, p; John Field, sb; Buzzy Drootin, d.

Storyville Club, Boston, Mass.	1953
Southie Is My Home Town	Storyville STLP307
Come Back Sweet Papa	Storyville STLP307
Jealous	Storyville STLP307
Muskrat Ramble	Storyville STLP307

WILBUR DE PARIS AND HIS "NEW" NEW ORLEANS JAZZ
Doc Cheatham, t; Sidney De Paris, t-1/tu-2; Wilbur De Paris, tb; Omer Simeon, cl; Sonny White, p; Lee Blair, bj; Wendell Marshall, sb; George Foster, d.

	New York City.	2 April 1955
1476	Mardi Gras -1	Atlantic SD1219
1477	Milneberg Joys -1	Atlantic SD1219
1479	Hot Lips -2	Atlantic SD1219

Doc Cheatham is not present on recording number 1478.

WILBUR DE PARIS AND HIS "NEW" NEW ORLEANS JAZZ
Doc Cheatham, t; Sidney De Paris, t-1/tu-2; Wilbur De Paris, tb; Omer Simeon, cl; Sonny White, p; Lee Blair, bj; Bennie Moten, sb; George Foster, d.

	New York City.	25 February 1957
2616	Easy To Love	Atlantic SD1288
2618	I've Got You Under My Skin	Atlantic SD1288
2619	I Get A Kick Out Of You	Atlantic SD1288
2620	Anything Goes	Atlantic SD1288
2623	It's All Right With Me	Atlantic SD1288

Doc Cheatham is not present on other recordings from this session.

COUNT BASIE ALL STARS
Doc Cheatham, Roy Eldridge, Joe Newman, Emmett Berry, t; Vic Dickenson, Dickie Wells, Frank Rehak, tb; Earle Warren, as; Lester Young, Coleman Hawkins, ts; Count Basie, p; Freddy Green, g; Eddie Jones, sb; Jo Jones, d; Jimmy Rushing, v-1.

	New York City.	5 December 1957
CO-59471	I Left My Baby -1	Columbia CL1098
CO-59472	Dickie's Dream	Columbia CL1098

BILLIE HOLIDAY with MAL WALDRON ALL STARS
Doc Cheatham, t; Vic Dickenson, tb; Lester Young, Coleman Hawkins, ts; Mal Waldron, p; Danny Barker, g; Jim Atlas, sb; Jo Jones, d.

	New York City.	5 December 1957
CO-59473	Fine And Mellow	Columbia CL1098

COUNT BASIE ALL STARS
Doc Cheatham, Roy Eldridge, Joe Newman, Emmett Berry, t; Vic Dickenson, Dickie Wells, Frank Rehak, tb; Earle Warren, as; Lester Young, Coleman Hawkins, ts; Count Basie, p; Freddy Green, g; Eddie Jones, sb; Jo Jones, d; Jimmy Rushing, v-1.

CBS Telecast, 'The Sound Of Jazz', New York City.	8 December 1957
Open All Night	Pumpkin 116
I Left My Baby -1	Pumpkin 116
Dickie's Dream	Extreme Rarities 1002

Open All Night is retitled *Fast And Happy Blues* on Pumpkin 116.

BILLIE HOLIDAY with MAL WALDRON ALL STARS
Doc Cheatham, Roy Eldridge, t; Vic Dickenson, tb; Lester Young, Coleman
Hawkins, Ben Webster, ts; Gerry Mulligan, bar; Mal Waldron, p; Danny
Barker, g; Milt Hinton, sb; Osie Johnson, d.

CBS Telecast, 'The Sound Of Jazz', New York City.	8 December 1957
Fine And Mellow	Everest FS310

JUANITA HALL acc. CLAUDE HOPKINS ORCHESTRA
Doc Cheatham, t; Buster Bailey, cl; Coleman Hawkins, ts; Claude Hopkins,
p; George Duvivier, sb; Jimmy Crawford, d; Juanita Hall, v.

New York City.	1958
I Don't Want It Second-Hand	Counterpoint CH564
You've Been A Good Old Wagon	Counterpoint CH564
Baby Won't You Please Come Home	Counterpoint CH564
Downhearted Blues	Counterpoint CH564
Gimme A Pigfoot	Counterpoint CH564
Nobody Knows You When You're Down And Out	Counterpoint CH564
Hold That Train	Counterpoint CH564
A Good Man Is Hard To Find	Counterpoint CH564
Gulf Coast Blues	Counterpoint CH564
I Ain't Gonna Play No Second Fiddle	Counterpoint CH564
Lovin' Sam From Alabam	Counterpoint CH564
After You've Gone	Counterpoint CH564

JIMMY RUSHING AND HIS ORCHESTRA

Doc Cheatham, Mel Davis, Buck Clayton, Emmett Berry, t; Frank Rehak,
Urbie Green, Dickie Wells, tb; Earle Warren, as; Rudy Powell, as/cl-2;
Buddy Tate, Coleman Hawkins, ts; Danny Bank, bar; Nat Pierce, p/cel-1;
Danny Barker, g; Milt Hinton, sb; Osie Johnson, d.

	New York City.	26 February 1958
CO-60476	Knock Me A Kiss -1	Columbia CL1152
CO-60477	Jimmy's Blues	Columbia CL1152
CO-60478	Someday Sweetheart -2	Columbia CL1152
CO-60479	Harvard Blues	Columbia CL1152
	New York City.	27 February 1958
CO-60480	It's A Sin To Tell A Lie	Columbia CL1152
CO-60481	Trav'lin' Light	Columbia CL1152
CO-60482	When You're Smiling	Columbia CL1152
CO-60483	Somebody Stole My Gal	Columbia CL1152

WILBUR DE PARIS AND HIS "NEW" NEW ORLEANS JAZZ

Sidney De Paris, Doc Cheatham, t; Wilbur De Paris, tb; Omer Simeon, cl;
Sonny White, p; Lee Blair, bj; Hayes Alvis, sb; Wilbert Kirk, d/h.

	New York City.	26 May 1958
3074	Bouquets	Atlantic SD1300
3075	Beale Street Blues	Atlantic SD1300

DOC CHEATHAM AND SAMMY PRICE

Doc Cheatham, t; Sammy Price, p.

Paris, France	October 1958
Lady Be Good	Club Français du Disque(F) 142
I Got Rhythm	Club Français du Disque(F) 142
Summertime	Club Français du Disque(F) 142
Embraceable You	Club Français du Disque(F) 142
Rhapsody In Blue	Club Français du Disque(F) 142

WILBUR DE PARIS AND HIS "NEW" NEW ORLEANS JAZZ

Sidney De Paris, Doc Cheatham, t; Wilbur De Paris, tb; Omer Simeon, cl;
Sonny White, p; Lee Blair, bj; Hayes Alvis, sb; Wilbert Kirk, d/h.

New York City. 15 December 1958

3235	Petite Fleur	Atlantic 2011
3236	Table Thumper's Rag	Atlantic unissued
3237	Over And Over Again	Atlantic 2011
3238	Colonel Bogey's March	Atlantic SD1300

WILBUR DE PARIS AND HIS "NEW" NEW ORLEANS JAZZ

Doc Cheatham, t; Wilbur De Paris, tb; Omer Simeon, cl; Rudy Rutherford,
cl/bar; Sonny White, p; John Smith, g; Hayes Alvis, sb; Wilbert Kirk, d/h.

New York City. 8 April 1959

3429	Majorca	Atlantic 2030
3430	Would You Care	Atlantic SD1552
3431	You Never Did Before	Atlantic unissued
3432	Watching Dreams Go By	Atlantic SD1552

Doc Cheatham, t; Wilbur De Paris, tb; Omer Simeon, cl; Sonny White, p;
John Smith, g; Hayes Alvis, sb; Wilbert Kirk, d/h.

Engineering Hall, New York City. 20 April 1959

3445	Malta	Atlantic SD1318
3446	Hesitatin' Blues	Atlantic SD1318
3447	That's A Plenty	Atlantic SD1318
3448	Change O' Key Boogie	Atlantic SD1318
3449	Mack The Knife	Atlantic SD1318

WILBUR DE PARIS AND HIS "NEW" NEW ORLEANS JAZZ

Sidney De Paris, c; Doc Cheatham, t; Wilbur De Paris, tb; Garvin Bushell,
cl; Sonny White, p/o; John Smith, bj/g; Hayes Alvis, sb; Wilbert Kirk, d/h.

New York City. 9 May 1960

4540	Minorca	Atlantic SD1336
4541	Creole Love Call	Atlantic SD1336
4542	Tell 'Em About Me	Atlantic SD1336
4543	Baby Won't You Please Come Home	Atlantic SD1336
4544	That Thing Called Love	Atlantic SD1336
4545	Railroad Man	Atlantic SD1336

New York City.		10 May 1960
4546	Twelfth Street Rag	Atlantic SD1336
4547	Shim-Me-Sha-Wabble	Atlantic SD1336
4548	When My Sugar Walks Down The Street	Atlantic SD1336
4549	Runnin' Wild	Atlantic SD1336
4550	The Charleston	Atlantic SD1336
4551	Blues Ingee	Atlantic SD1336

WILBUR DE PARIS AND HIS "NEW" NEW ORLEANS JAZZ

Sidney De Paris, c; Doc Cheatham, t; Wilbur De Paris, tb; Garvin Bushell, cl; Sonny White, p/o; John Smith, bj/g; Hayes Alvis, sb; Wilbert Kirk, d/h.

Antibes, France.		10 July 1960
5266	Fidgety Feet	Atlantic SD1363
5267	Tres Moutarde	Atlantic SD1363
5268	Malta	Atlantic unissued
5269	St. Louis Blues	Atlantic SD1363
5270	South Rampart Street Parade	Atlantic SD1363
5271	Sensation	Atlantic SD1363
5272	Jam Session	Atlantic unissued
5273	Sweet Georgia Brown	Atlantic unissued
5274	I Found A New Baby	Atlantic unissued
5275	Royal Garden Blues	Atlantic unissued
5276	Minorca	Atlantic unissued
5277	Tell Them About Me	Atlantic unissued
5278	Charleston	Atlantic unissued
5279	12th Street Rag	Atlantic unissued
5280	Flow Gently Sweet Afton	Atlantic unissued
5281	That's A Plenty	Atlantic unissued
5282	Minorca	Atlantic unissued
5283	The Blues In G	Atlantic unissued
5284	Clarinet Marmalade	Atlantic SD1363
5285	Muskrat Ramble	Atlantic SD1363
5286	Battle Hymn Of The Republic	Atlantic SD1363

These recordings were made by Barclay(F) and sold to Atlantic.

HERBIE MANN

Doc Cheatham, Leo Ball, Ziggy Schatz, Jerry Kail, t; Herbie Mann, fl; Johnny Rae, vb; Knobby Totah, b; Rudy Collins, d-1; Ray Barretto, Ray

Mantilla, Michael Olatunji, perc.

New York City.		1960
	I'll Remember April -1	Verve MGV8392
	Dearly Beloved	Verve MGV8392
	Stretch Out (You Stepped Out Of A Dream) -1	
		Verve MGV8392
	A Ritual -1	Verve MGV8392
	Fife 'N' Tambourine Corp. -1	Verve MGV8392
	Autumn Leaves -1	Verve MGV8392

New York City.		2 August 1960
4761	Walkin' -1	Atlantic SD1343
4762	St. Thomas -1	Atlantic SD1343

Doc Cheatham is not present on 4763 *Night In Tunisia* from this session. *Walkin'* was subsequently re-mastered into Pt. 1 & Pt. 2 under master numbers 5398/99 and issued thus on Atlantic 5010 (45 r.p.m. SP).

HERBIE MANN
Doc Cheatham, Leo Ball, Ziggy Schatz, Jerry Kail, t; Herbie Mann, fl; Johnny Rae, vb; Knobby Totah, b; Rudy Collins, d; Ray Barretto, Ray Mantilla, Michael Olatunji, perc; Maya Angelou, Dolores Parker, v.

New York City.		3 August 1960
4780	Baghdad, Asia Minor	Atlantic SD1343
4781	The Common Ground	Atlantic SD1343
4782	High Life (Happy Brass)	Atlantic 5009
		(45 SP), SD1343
4785	Lotati	Atlantic unissued

Some of these titles were re-recorded on 4 August 1960. Doc Cheatham is not present on 4783 *Uhuru*, and 4784 *Sawa Sawa Dé*, from these sessions.

WILBUR DE PARIS AND HIS "NEW" NEW ORLEANS JAZZ
Sidney De Paris, t/tu; Doc Cheatham, t; Wilbur De Paris, tb; Garvin Bushell, cl/bsn; Sonny White, p; John Smith, bj/g; Hayes Alvis, sb; Wilbert Kirk, d/h.

New York City.		16 November 1960
5173	How Ya Gonna Keep 'Em Down On The Farm	
		Atlantic SD1552
5174	Wabash Blues	Atlantic SD1552
5175	Ja-Da	Atlantic SD1552

| 5176 | Royal Garden Blues | Atlantic SD1552 |

	New York City.	17 November 1960
5187	Over And Over Again (Version I)	Atlantic SD1552
5188	Careless Love	Atlantic SD1552
5189	Just A Closer Walk With Thee	Atlantic SD1552
5190	Goodnight Irene	Atlantic SD1552

SHORTY BAKER-DOC CHEATHAM

Harold 'Shorty' Baker, Doc Cheatham, t; Walter Bishop, Jr., p; Wendell Marshall, sb; J.C. Heard, d.

	New York City.	17 January 1961
2827	Baker's Dozen	Swingville SVLP2021
2828	Night Train	Swingville SVLP2021
2829	Lullabye In Rhythm *[sic]*	Swingville SVLP2021
2831	Chitlin's	Swingville SVLP2021
2832	Good Queen Bess	Swingville SVLP2021

Doc Cheatham is not present on 2830 *I Didn't Know What Time It Was.*

LEONARD GASKIN'S ALL STARS

Doc Cheatham, t; Yank Lawson, t-1; Vic Dickenson, tb; Cutty Cutshall, tb-1; Buster Bailey, cl; Edmond Hall, cl-1; Dick Wellstood, p; Leonard Gaskin, sb; Herbie Lovelle, d.

	New York City.	30 November 1961
	At The Jazz Band Ball -1	Swingville SVLP2031
	Mack The Knife	Swingville SVLP2031
	Hindustan	Swingville SVLP2031

DOC CHEATHAM With THE BLUE NOTES

| | Tokyo, Japan. | 1965 |
| | unknown titles | unknown label(J) |

Doc Cheatham recalls making this album while touring with Machito and His Orchestra, but details have not been located.

BENNY GOODMAN QUINTET
Doc Cheatham, t; Benny Goodman, cl; Hank Jones, p; Al Hall, sb; Morey Feld, d; Annette Saunders, v-1.

Rainbow Grill, New York City (WNEW broadcast). 19 May 1966

Indiana	Ombrads 2903
Cheerful Little Earful -1	Ombrads 2903
It's A Most Unusual Day -1	Ombrads 2903
A Handful Of Keys	Ombrads 2903

Doc Cheatham, t; Benny Goodman, cl; Herbie Hancock, p; Les Spann, g; Al Hall, sb; Morey Feld, d; Annette Saunders, v-1.

Rainbow Grill, New York City.   3/4 June 1966

Avalon	Musicmasters 5047-2-C (CD)
Embraceable You	Musicmasters 5047-2-C (CD)
Sweet Georgia Brown	Musicmasters 5047-2-C (CD)
Look For The Silver Lining -1	Musicmasters 5047-2-C (CD)
By Myself	Musicmasters 5047-2-C (CD)
Honeysuckle Rose	Musicmasters 5047-2-C (CD)

CAP'N JOHN HANDY with CLAUDE HOPKINS' ORCHESTRA
Doc Cheatham, t; Benny Morton, tb; Scoville Brown, cl/ts; John Handy, as; Claude Hopkins, p; Eddie Gibbs, sb; Gus Johnson, d.

New York City.   15 November 1966

TPA1-8635	While We Danced At The Mardi Gras	RCA-Victor LPMS3762
TPA1-8636	Bourbon Street Strut	RCA-Victor LPMS3762
TPA1-8637	I Would Do Most Anything For You	RCA-Victor LPMS3762

New York City.		16 November 1966
TPA1-8639	Baby Won't You Please Come Home	RCA-Victor LPMS3762
TPA1-8640	Handy's Gulf Coast Boogie	RCA-Victor LPMS3762
TPA1-8641	Cabaret	RCA-Victor LPMS3762

New York City.		17 November 1966
TPA1-8643	Pass The Ribs	RCA-Victor LPMS3762
TPA1-8645	One O'Clock Jump	RCA-Victor LPMS3762
TPA1-8646	Perdido	RCA-Victor LPMS3762

New York City.		18 November 1966
TPA1-8650	Good Feeling Blues	RCA-Victor LPMS3762
TPA1-8652	I Laughed At Love	RCA-Victor LPMS3762

HAYES ALVIS' PIONEERS OF JAZZ
Doc Cheatham, t; Clyde Bernhardt, tb/v-1; Herb Hall, cl; Jimmy Evans, p; Hayes Alvis, sb; Wilbert Kirk, d.

Meriden, Conn.	18 March 1972
St. Louis Blues -1	CTJC SLP8
Old Fashioned Love	CTJC SLP8
Royal Garden Blues	CTJC SLP8

DICK WELLSTOOD ALL STARS
Doc Cheatham, t; Vic Dickenson, tb; Kenny Davern, cl-1/ss-2; Dick Wellstood, p; George Duvivier, sb; Gus Johnson, d.

New York City.	c. 1972
Way Down Yonder In New Orleans -2	Music Minus One 4090/3
Red Sails In The Sunset -1	Music Minus One 4090/3

Second-Hand Rose -2	Music Minus One 4090/3
Royal Garden Blues -1,2	Music Minus One 4090/3
Rose Of Washington Square -2	Music Minus One 4090/3
Sunny Side Of The Street -1,2	Music Minus One 4090/3
I Want A Little Girl -2	Music Minus One 4090/3
Exactly Like You -2	Music Minus One 4090/3

Band name not known
Doc Cheatham, t; Benny Morton, tb; Earle Warren, as; Ellis Larkins, p; Milt Hinton, sb; Jo Jones, d.

New York City.   18 October 1972

Untitled Blues	Black Lion unissued
I've Got The World On A String	Black Lion unissued
Swinging The Blues	Black Lion unissued
St. Louis Blues	Black Lion unissued
Summertime	Black Lion unissued

There was no titular leader on this session, which was recorded by Albert McCarthy.

ADOLPHUS 'DOC' CHEATHAM
Doc Cheatham, t; Jimmy Andrews, p; Tom Anthony, sb; Mike Burgevin, d.

New York City.   4 April 1973

Don't Worry 'Bout Me	Jezebel JZ102
It Had To Be You	Jezebel JZ102
Liza	Jezebel JZ102
Days Of Wine And Roses	Jezebel JZ102
Broadway	Jezebel JZ102

Gee Baby Ain't I Good To You	Jezebel JZ102
Mandy Make Up Your Mind	Jezebel JZ102

New York City.   5 April 1973

Tin Roof Blues	Jezebel JZ102
Lullaby In Rhythm	Jezebel JZ102
Deep Purple	Jezebel JZ102
As Time Goes By	Jezebel JZ102
If Dreams Come True	Jezebel JZ102
Manhattan	Jezebel JZ102

New York City.   9 April 1973

That's All	Jezebel JZ102
When My Baby Smiles At Me	Jezebel JZ102
La Vie En Rose	Jezebel JZ102
This Is All I Ask	Jezebel JZ102
Bugle Call Rag	Jezebel JZ102
Caution Blues	Jezebel JZ102
Blue Room	Jezebel JZ102

The last title is thought to come from this session but was omitted from the information given in the original notes, so might rather come from either of the previous sessions.

EARLE WARREN AND THE COUNT'S MEN

Doc Cheatham, t; Al Cobbs, tb-1; Earle Warren, as-1; Harry Porter, ts-1; Chuck Folds, p; Franklin Skeete, sb; Ronnie Cole, d.

New York City.   12 July 1973

Blue Boy -1	RCA(E) LFL1-5034
Curly Top -1	RCA(E) LFL1-5034
I Want A Little Girl	RCA(E) LFL1-5034
We're Rollin' -1	RCA(E) unissued
Earle's Blues -1	RCA(E) LFL1-5067

Doc Cheatham does not play on *Something* from this session.

CLYDE BERNHARDT—JAY COLE HARLEM BLUES AND JAZZ BAND

Doc Cheatham, t; Clyde Bernhardt, tb/v-1; Charlie Holmes, as; Reuben Jay Cole, p; Barbara Dreiwitz, tu; Tommy Benford, d; Miss Rhapsody (Viola Wells), v-2.

New York City.   10 November 1973

Frankie And Johnny -1	400 W.150 VLP400
Squeeze Me -1	400 W.150 VLP400
Stagolee -1	400 W.150 VLP400
You Don't Know My Mind -1	400 W.150 VLP400
Sweet Man -2	400 W.150 VLP400
My Lucky Day -2	400 W.150
	unissued
After You've Gone -2	400 W.150
	unissued
I'm Satisfied -2	400 W.150
	unissued
Bye Bye Blues -2	400 W.150
	unissued

New York City.	20 November 1973
Please Don't Talk About Me When I'm Gone	
	400 W.150 VLP400
Tishomingo Blues	400 W.150 VLP400
She's Got What I Need	400 W.150 VLP400
Washington And Lee Swing	Barron VLP403
Mahogany Hall Stomp	Barron VLP403
Ballin' The Jack	Barron VLP403

Barron VLP403 as by **THE HARLEM BLUES AND JAZZ BAND**

DOC CHEATHAM AND HIS ORCHESTRA
Doc Cheatham, t; Joe Muranyi, cl/as; Gloria Hearn, ep/v; Al Casey, g; Al Hall, sb; Irwin Spivak, d.

Bayside, N.Y.	December 1973
Jam On Blues	Jazz Ways
	FW106/2
I Can't Believe That You're In Love With Me	Jazz Ways
	FW106/2
Ain't Misbehavin'	Jazz Ways
	FW106/2
There'll Be Some Changes Made	Jazz Ways
	FW106/2
Satin Doll	Jazz Ways

110

	FW106/2
Sugar	Jazz Ways
	FW106/2
On A Clear Day	Jazz Ways
	FW106/2

EARL HINES SEXTET

Doc Cheatham, t; Rudy Rutherford, cl/as/ts; Earl Hines, p; Jack Wilkins, g;
Jimmy Leary, sb; Ray Mosca, d.

New York City.	5 December 1973
Bright Attitude	Black Lion
	BLP30190
Le Bijou	Black Lion
	BLP30190
You Can Depend On Me	Black Lion
	BLP30190
Swingin' Away	Black Lion
	BLP30190
Senator Sam	Black Lion
	BLP30190
Rosetta	Black Lion
	BLP30190

New York City.	7 December 1973
Don't Take Your Love From Me	Black Lion
	BLP30190
Blue Lion Blues	Black Lion
	BLP30190

VIC DICKENSON SEXTET

Doc Cheatham, t; Vic Dickenson, tb; Zoot Sims, ts; Red Richards, p; John
'Bucky' Pizzarelli, g-1; Bill Pemberton, sb; Oliver Jackson, d.

New York City.		15 February 1974
take 1	D. B. Blues -1	RCA(E) LFL1-5032
take 2	D. B. Blues -1	RCA(E) LFL1-5036
	Nancy	RCA(E) LFL1-5036
	I Want You	RCA(E) LFL1-5036

Doc Cheatham is not present on *Cuddle Up A Little Closer* from this
session.

JANE HARVEY

Doc Cheatham, t; Don Elliott, vb-1; John Bunch, p; John 'Bucky' Pizzarelli, g; Richard Davis, sb; Bill Goodwin, d; Jane Harvey, v.

New York City.	20 February 1974
Do Do Do	RCA(E) LPL1-5030
When A Woman Loves A Man	RCA(E) LPL1-5030
I've Got The World On A String -1	RCA(E) LPL1-5031

BUCK CLAYTON JAM SESSION

Doc Cheatham, Joe Newman, t; Urbie Green, tb; Earle Warren, as; Budd Johnson, ts/ss; Zoot Sims, ts; Joe Temperley, bar; Earl Hines, p; Milt Hinton, sb; Gus Johnson, d; Buck Clayton, a.

New York City.	25/26 March 1974
Boss Blues	Chiaroscuro CR132
Case Closed	Chiaroscuro CR132
Easy Blue	Chiaroscuro CR132
Jayhawk	Chiaroscuro CR163

BEAVER HARRIS 360° MUSIC EXPERIENCE

Doc Cheatham, t; Marshall Brown, tb/euph; Herb Hall, cl; Dave Burrell, p; Jimmy Garrison, sb-1; Ron Carter, sb-2; Beaver Harris, d; Maxine Sullivan, v-3.

New York City.	20 January & 11 February 1975
Can Here Be Peace -1, 3	360° Music 2001
It's Hard But We Do -2	360° Music 2001
I Wish I Knew -1, 3	360° Music 2001

SAMMY PRICE

Doc Cheatham, t; Gene 'Mighty Flea' Conners, tb; Ted Buckner, as; Sammy Price, p; Carl Pruitt, sb; J.C. Heard, d.

Paris.	1 May 1975
West End Boogie	Black & Blue(F) 33.079
Whodat Blues	Black & Blue(F) 33.079
Riffin' Boogie	Black & Blue(F) 33.079

'Tain't Nobody's Bizzness   Black & Blue(F)
33.079

DOC CHEATHAM

Doc Cheatham, t/v-1; Gene 'Mighty Flea' Conners, tb; Ted Buckner, as;
Sammy Price, p; Carl Pruitt, sb; J.C. Heard, d.

    Paris.   2 May 1975

         Rosetta   Black & Blue(F)
33.090

         Blues In My Heart   Black & Blue(F)
33.090

         What Can I Say After I Say I'm Sorry -1   Black & Blue(F)
33.090

         Saint James Infirmary   Black & Blue(F)
33.090

         Sugar   Black & Blue(F)
33.090

         If I Could Be With You (One Hour) -1   Black & Blue(F)
33.090

         Rose Room   Black & Blue(F)
33.090

Doc Cheatham, t; Sammy Price, p.

    Paris.   2 May 1975

         I Cover The Waterfront   Black & Blue(F)
33.090

SAMMY PRICE (33.560, 233.079)/J.C. HEARD SEXTET (59.080-2)/DOC CHEATHAM (59.090-2)

Doc Cheatham, t; Gene 'Mighty Flea' Conners, tb; Ted Buckner, as; Sammy
Price, p; Carl Pruitt, sb; J.C. Heard, d; Marie Buggs, v-2

    Paris.   12 May 1975

         Squeeze Me   Black & Blue(F)
33.560

         Boogie With Riffs   Black & Blue(F)
33.560

         I Want A Little Girl -1   Black & Blue(F)
33.560

Cocktails For Two	Black & Blue(F) 33.560
Last Boogie	Black & Blue(F) 33.560
Rockin' Boogie	Black & Blue(F) 33.560
What Can I Say After I Say I'm Sorry -1	Black & Blue(F) 33.560
Willow Weep For Me	Black & Blue(F) 33.560
Empty Bed Blues -2	Black & Blue(F) 33.560
Backwater Blues -2	Black & Blue(F) 33.560

Toulouse, France.   20 May 1975

Ain't She Sweet	Black & Blue(F) 233.079 (CD)
Blues For Dr. Bonte	Black & Blue(F) 233.079 (CD)

Toulouse, France.   21 May 1975

For You My Love	Black & Blue(F) 233.079 (CD)
Muskrat Ramble	Black & Blue(F) 233.079 (CD)
Cute	Black & Blue(F) 59.080-2 (CD)
Ain't Misbehavin'	Black & Blue(F) 59.090-2 (CD)

BUDDY TATE—DOC CHEATHAM—VIC DICKENSON (Mahogany)

or BUDDY TATE ALL STARS (Storyville)

Doc Cheatham, t; Vic Dickenson, tb-1; Buddy Tate, ts-2; Johnny Guarnieri, p; George Duvivier, sb; Oliver Jackson, d.

Antibes, France.   23 July 1975

Jive At Five -1, 2	Mahogany(F) 558.103

Jive At Five (alt. take) -1, 2	Storyville (Da)STCD5010 (CD)
Somebody Loves Me -1, 2	Mahogany(F) 558.103
Sweethearts On Parade -1, 2	Mahogany(F) 558.103
I Gotta Right To Sing The Blues	Mahogany(F) 558.103
I Never Knew -1, 2	Mahogany(F) 558.103
Somebody Loves Me -1, 2	Storyville (Da)STCD5010 (CD)

Doc Cheatham does not appear on *There Goes My Heart* and *Constantly* from this session.

CLYDE BERNHARDT AND THE HARLEM BLUES AND JAZZ BAND
Doc Cheatham, t; Clyde Bernhardt, tb; George James, as; Jimmy Evans, p; Barbara Dreiwitz, tu; Tommy Benford, d; Princess White (Durrah), v.
New York City.   16 September 1975

Sittin' On Top Of The World	Barron VLP401
Every Woman's Blues	Barron VLP401
Old Fashioned Love	Barron unissued

Doc Cheatham, t; Franc Williams, t/fh; Clyde Bernhardt, tb; George James, as/ss; Charlie Holmes, as-1; Dill Jones, p; Barbara Dreiwitz, tu; Tommy Benford, d.
New York City.   9 October 1975

Careless Love -1	Barron VLP401
Bugle Call Rag	Barron VLP401
Somebody Stole My Gal -1	Barron VLP401

THE COUNTSMEN
Doc Cheatham, t; Benny Morton, tb; Earle Warren, as/cl/v; Buddy Tate, ts/cl; Dill Jones, p; Franklin Skeete, sb; Ronnie Cole, d.
Newington, Conn.   25 October 1975

Moten Swing	CTJC SLP12

JIM BARTOW
Doc Cheatham, t; Vic Dickenson, tb-1; Jim Bartow, g/v; Larry Lucie, g-2;
Bill Ellington, sb; Panama Francis, d.

New York City.	c. 1975
Away -1, 2	Blues Blood BB132
E.D.'s Blues	Blues Blood BB132
Blues Enuff -1	Blues Blood BB132

Doc Cheatham is not on other titles from this album.

HERB HALL/DOC CHEATHAM ALL STARS
Doc Cheatham, t; Vic Dickenson, tb; Herb Hall, cl; Red Richards, p; Bill
Crow, sb; Jackie Williams, d.

Meriden, Conn.	24 January 1976
Please Don't Talk About Me When I've Gone	
	CTJC SLP12
Creole Love Song	CTJC SLP12

CARRIE SMITH
Doc Cheatham, t; Vic Dickenson, tb; Eddie Barefield, cl/ts; Sir Charles
Thompson, p; George Duvivier, sb; Panama Francis, d; Carrie Smith, v.

Barcelona, Spain.	26 July 1976
Don't Be That Way	Black & Blue 33.103
'Deed I Do	Black & Blue 33.103
Please Send Me Someone To Love	Black & Blue 33.103
Careless Love (take 1)	Black & Blue 233.119 (CD)
Careless Love	Black & Blue 33.103
Give Your Mama One Smile	Black & Blue 33.103
Everybody Loves My Baby (take 1)	Black & Blue 233.119 (CD)
Everybody Loves My Baby	Black & Blue 33.103
I Cried For You	Black & Blue 33.103
Do Your Duty	Black & Blue 33.103
Do Your Duty (alt. take)	Black & Blue 233.119 (CD)
All Of Me	Black & Blue 33.103

116

DOC CHEATHAM—SAMMY PRICE
Doc Cheatham, t; Sammy Price, p.

Toronto, Canada.	17 November 1976
Honeysuckle Rose	Sackville(Ca) 3013
Doc And Sam's Blues	Sackville(Ca) 3013
Summertime	Sackville(Ca) 3013
Tishomingo Blues	Sackville(Ca) 3013
The Sheik Of Araby	Sackville(Ca) 3013
I Can't Give You Anything But Love	Sackville(Ca) 3013
You Can Depend On Me	Sackville(Ca) 3013
Ain't Misbehavin'	Sackville(Ca) 3013
Dear Old Southland	Sackville(Ca) 3013

HARLEM ON PARADE 77
Doc Cheatham, Dick Vance, t; Eddie Barefield, as; Buddy Tate, ts; Budd Johnson, ts/ss; Hank Jones, p; Bill Pemberton, sb; Oliver Jackson, d; Carrie Smith, v-1.

Miraval, France.	19 July 1977
Doc And Dick	Black & Blue(F) 33.159
Oliver's Moments	Black & Blue(F) 33.159
Budd And Buddy Blues	Black & Blue(F) 33.159
Yesterdays	Black & Blue(F) 33.159
Silver And Gold	Black & Blue(F) 33.159
Ill Wind -1	Black & Blue(F) 33.159
When I Been Drinking -1	Black & Blue(F) 33.159

LIONEL HAMPTON ALL STAR BAND
Doc Cheatham, t; Cat Anderson, Jimmy Maxwell, Joe Newman, t/fh; Eddie Bert, John Gordon, Benny Powell, tb; Bob Wilber, cl; Earle Warren, cl/f/ss; Charles McPherson, as; Paul Moen, Arnett Cobb, ts; Pepper Adams, bar; Lionel Hampton, vb; Ray Bryant, p; Teddy Wilson, p-1; Billy Mackel, g;

117

Chubby Jackson, sb; Panama Francis, d.

Carnegie Hall, New York City.	1 July 1978
Hamp's Boogie Woogie	Sultra SU2-1006
Tea For Two -1	Sultra SU2-1006
I'm Confessin' That I Love You	Sultra SU2-1006
Misty	Sultra SU2-1006
Avalon -1	Sultra SU2-1006
More Than You Know -1	Sultra SU2-1006
Runnin' Wild -1	Sultra SU2-1006
Carnegie Hall, New York City.	2 July 1978
Stompin' At the Savoy	Timeless(Du) SJP142
On The Sunny Side Of The Street	Timeless(Du) SJP142
Hamp's The Champ	Timeless(Du) SJP142
Carnegie Hall Blues	Timeless(Du) SJP142
Flying Home	Timeless(Du) SJP142

This session was recorded by Nippon Phonogram and they may have issued it first but their issue number is not known.

JAY McSHANN

Doc Cheatham, t; Dickie Wells, tb; Earle Warren, as; Herbie Mann, ts/cl; Jay McShann, p/v-1; John Scofield, g; Eddie Gomez, sb-2; Milt Hinton, sb-3; Connie Kay, d; Janis Siegel, v-4.

New York City.	3/8/10 August 1978
Dickie's Dream -3	Atlantic SD8804
Ain't Misbehavin' -2, 4	Atlantic SD8804
Blue Feeling -2	Atlantic SD8804
Jumpin' The Blues -3	Atlantic SD8804

NATALIE LAMB

Doc Cheatham, t; Sammy Price, p; Candy McDonald, d; Natalie Lamb, v.

Unknown location	c. 1979
My Daddy Rocks Me	G.H.B. GHB84
Backwater Blues	G.H.B. GHB84

Gimme A Pigfoot	G.H.B. GHB84
Make Me A Pallet On The Floor	G.H.B. GHB84
'T Ain't Nobody's Business If I Do	G.H.B. GHB84
I Need A Little Sugar	G.H.B. GHB84
Oh Papa	G.H.B. GHB84
Jazzin' Baby Blues	G.H.B. GHB84
Frosty Mornin' Blues	G.H.B. GHB84
St. Louis Blues	G.H.B. GHB84

DOC CHEATHAM

Doc Cheatham, t/v; Ellis Larkins, p; Milt Hinton, sb; Oliver Jackson, d.

New York City.		17 February 1979
E1012-A	Laura	Jazz Session JS6
		(45 SP)

Max Kaminsky, c/t; Doc Cheatham, t; Benny Morton, tb; Herb Hall, cl; Dill Jones, p; Brian Torff, sb; Ronnie Cole, d.

New York City.		17 February 1979
C1050	That Da Da Strain	Jazz Session JS6
		(45 SP)

FESSOR'S NIGHTHAWKS

Doc Cheatham, t; Ole 'Fessor' Lindgreen, tb; Herb Hall, cl; Steen Vig, ts; Hans Otto Jørgensen, p; Leif Bjerborg, g; John Williams, sb; Thorkild Møller, d.

Copenhagen, Denmark.	20 August 1979
Hefty Jazz	Metronome(Sd) MELP627
Little Happy Caldwell	Metronome(Sd) MELP627
Charlie's Boogie	Metronome(Sd) MELP627
Four O'Clock Drag	Metronome(Sd) MELP627
Sometimes	Metronome(Sd) MELP627
Doc's Lullaby	Metronome(Sd) MELP627

119

DOC CHEATHAM—SAMMY PRICE
Doc Cheatham, t; Sammy Price, p.

Toronto, Canada.	31 October 1979
Travelin' All Alone	Sackville(Ca) 3029
Some Of These Days	Sackville(Ca) 3029
Love Will Find A Way	Sackville(Ca) 3029
After You've Gone	Sackville(Ca) 3029
Someday You'll Be Sorry	Sackville(Ca) 3029
Old Fashioned Love	Sackville(Ca) 3029
I'm Coming Virginia	Sackville(Ca) 3029
Squeeze Me	Sackville(Ca) 3029
Memphis Blues	Sackville(Ca) 3029
I've Got A Feeling I'm Falling	Sackville(Ca) 3029
Louisiana	Sackville(Ca) 3029

BIG CHIEF RUSSELL MOORE ALL STAR JAZZ BAND
Doc Cheatham, t; 'Big Chief' Russell Moore, tb/v-1; Eddie Barefield, cl; Marty Napoleon, p; Al Hall, sb; Buddy Christian, d.

Meriden, Conn.	c. 1980
How Long Blues -1	CTJC CLP17
Avalon	CTJC CLP17

DOC CHEATHAM, FRANZ JACKSON AND THE JAZZ ENTERTAINERS
Doc Cheatham, t/v; Franz Jackson, ts/v; Graeme Bell, p; Arie Lighthart, g; Bob van Oven, sb; Martin Beenen, d.

Congresshall of the Turfschip, Breda, Netherlands	May 1981
It Don't Mean A Thing	Jazz Crooner(Du) JC283181

ADOLPHUS "DOC" CHEATHAM
Doc Cheatham, t; with Hot Jazz Orchestra Of New York: Joel Hellany, Dan Barrett, tb; Joe Muranyi, as/ts/cl; Dill Jones, p; Howard Alden, g; Milt Hinton, sb; Jake Hanna, d; Cynthia Sayer, v-1; Lew Micallef, v-2; Eddy Davis, v-3.

New York City.	25/26 October 1982
It's Been So Long	New York Jazz J002
East St. Louis Toodle-Oo	New York Jazz J002
Let's Do It -1	New York Jazz J002
Procurement	New York Jazz J002

Smith Here	New York Jazz J002
Too Marvelous For Words -2	New York Jazz J002
Blues In The Night	New York Jazz J002
It's That Great Basie Band -3	New York Jazz J002
Indiana	New York Jazz J003
Upstairs With "The Judge"	New York Jazz J003
It's That Great Basie Band	New York Jazz J003
Hoosier Hunch	New York Jazz J003

Doc Cheatham, t/v; Howard Alden, g.
  Same sessions.

I've Got A Crush On You	New York Jazz J003
I'd Do Most Anything For You	New York Jazz J003
It's Been A Long, Long Time	New York Jazz J003
Squeeze Me	New York Jazz J003

JIMMY RYAN'S NEW YORK ALL STARS
Doc Cheatham, t; Bob Pring, tb; Arnie Baker, cl; Johnny Morris, p; Willie Wayman, sb; Ernie Hackett, d.

North Haven, Conn.	20 November 1982
That's A Plenty	CTJC CLP19

OLD SCHOOL BAND
Jacques Lucas, c; Doc Cheatham, t; Eberhardt Nolte, tb; Reynold 'Pops' Gysin, cl; François Pesse, p; Jean-Claude Pesse, bj; Freddy Cotting, sb; Thierry Schell, d.

Geneva, Switzerland.	14 October 1983
Rosetta	Old School Band(Ss) 03
Jubilee	Old School Band(Ss) 03

DOC CHEATHAM AND HIS NEW YORK QUARTET
Doc Cheatham, t/v; Chuck Folds, p; Al Hall, sb; Jackie Williams, d.

New York City.	6/7 December 1982
Struttin' With Some Barbecue	Parkwood(Ca) PW101
She's Funny That Way	Parkwood(Ca) PW101

It Don't Mean A Thing	Parkwood(Ca) PW101
Peggy	Parkwood(Ca) PW101
The Good Life	Parkwood(Ca) PW101
Ring Dem Bells	Parkwood(Ca) PW101
You're Lucky To Me	Parkwood(Ca) PW101
St. Louis Blues	Parkwood(Ca) PW101

DOC CHEATHAM AND JIM GALLOWAY
Doc Cheatham, t; Roy Williams, tb; Jim Galloway, ss; Ian Bargh, p; Neil Swainson, sb; Terry Clarke, d.

Bern Jazz Festival, Switzerland.   30 April 1983

Cherry	Sackville(Ca) CD2-3045 (CD)
Creole Love Call	Sackville(Ca) CD2-3045 (CD)
Limehouse Blues	Sackville(Ca) CD2-3045 (CD)
Love Is Just Around The Corner	Sackville(Ca) CD2-3045 (CD)

Medley: Polka Dots And Moonbeams/When

| It's Sleepy Time Down South | Sackville(Ca) CD2-3045 (CD) |
| Way Down Yonder In New Orleans | Sackville(Ca) CD2-3045 (CD) |

DOC CHEATHAM
Doc Cheatham, t/v; Dick Wellstood, p; Bill Pemberton, sb; Jackie Williams, d.

New York City.   16/17 November 1983

| Big Butter And Egg Man | Parkwood(Ca) PW104 |

Deed I Do	Parkwood(Ca) PW104
Let's Do It (Let's Fall In Love)	Parkwood(Ca) PW104
The Man I Love	Parkwood(Ca) PW104
Swing That Music	Parkwood(Ca) PW104
'Round Midnight	Parkwood(Ca) PW104
Jeepers Creepers	Parkwood(Ca) PW104
I Double Dare You	Parkwood(Ca) PW104
Medley: Flee As A Bird/St. James Infirmary	
	Parkwood(Ca) PW104

MAXINE SULLIVAN

Doc Cheatham, t; Herb Hall, cl; Red Richards, p; Johnny Haynes, sb; Tom Martin, d; Maxine Sullivan, v.

Charlotte, N.C.	c. late 1983
I'm Beginning To See The Light	Audiophile AP185
I Thought About You	Audiophile AP185
Between The Devil And The Deep Blue Sea	
	Audiophile AP185
I Got It Bad And That Ain't Good	Audiophile AP185
Brother Can You Spare A Dime?	Audiophile AP185
Georgia On My Mind	Audiophile AP185
Don't Get Around Much Anymore	Audiophile AP185
Skylark	Audiophile AP185
What Is There To Say?	Audiophile AP185
I Didn't Know About You	Audiophile AP185
Just One Of Those Things	Audiophile AP185

DOC CHEATHAM AND JIM GALLOWAY
Doc Cheatham, t; Jim Galloway, ss; Ian Bargh, p; Neil Swainson, sb; Terry Clarke, d.
> Traders Lounge, Sheraton Hotel,Toronto, Canada. 17 May 1984
>> My Buddy   Sackville(Ca)
>>   CD2-3045 (CD)

DOC CHEATHAM
Doc Cheatham, t/v; Marcel Hendricks, p.
> Breda, Netherlands.   2 June 1984
>> Someday You'll Be Sorry   Jazz Crooner(Du)
>>   JC13684

SIDEWALK HOT JAZZ ORCHESTRA
Doc Cheatham, Erich Heidelberg, t; Norbert Schuster, tb; Gerhard Kron, as/ss/ts; Knut Drossé, p; Martin Schöning, bj/g; Joe Tarto, tu; Klaus Dau, sb; Jörg Möller, d.
> Breda, Netherlands.   3 June 1984
>> When It's Sleepy Time Down South   Jazz Crooner(Du)
>>   JC13684

DOC CHEATHAM AND JIM GALLOWAY
Doc Cheatham, t; Jim Galloway, ss; Ian Bargh, p; Neil Swainson, sb; Terry Clarke, d.
> Traders Lounge, Sheraton Hotel, Toronto, Canada. 5 January 1985
>> Street Of Dreams   Sackville(Ca) CD2-
>>   3045 (CD)
>> Swing That Music   Sackville(Ca) CD2-
>>   3045 (CD)

HIGHLIGHTS IN JAZZ
Doc Cheatham, t/v-1; Glenn Zottola, t; Phil Bodner, cl; Loren Schoenberg, ts; Marty Napoleon, p; Major Holley, sb; Butch Miles, d-2; Ray Mosca, d-3; Carrie Smith, v-4.
> Highlights In Jazz 12th Anniversary Concert, New York City.
>>   February 1985
>> Sweet Georgia Brown -3   Stash ST254
>> You're Lucky To Me -1, 3   Stash ST254
>> After You've Gone -2   Stash ST254

It's Love I'm After -2, 4	Stash ST254
Just You, Just Me -2	Stash ST254
St. Louis Blues -2	Stash ST254
Stardust -1	Stash ST254
Blues In The Night -1, 2, 4	Stash ST254

THE AUTHENTIC ART HODES RHYTHM SECTION ACCOMPANIES CARRIE SMITH WITH DOC CHEATHAM

Doc Cheatham, t; Art Hodes, p; Carrie Smith, v.

New York City.	7 June 1985
Back Water Blues	Parkwood(Ca) PW106
Maybe Not At All (Not On The First Night Baby)	Parkwood(Ca) PW106
Wasted Life Blues	Parkwood(Ca) PW106
Big Butter And Egg Man	Parkwood(Ca) PW106

Doc Cheatham, t; Art Hodes, p; Carrie Smith, v-1.

New York City.	8 June 1985
Jelly Roll Blues	Parkwood(Ca) PW106
When It's Sleepy Time Down South	Parkwood(Ca) PW106
You Rascal You (I'll Be Glad When You're Dead) -1	Parkwood(Ca) PW106
There'll Be Some Changes Made	Parkwood(Ca) PW106

DOC CHEATHAM AND GEORGE KELLY (Highlights In Jazz Anniversary Concert)

Doc Cheatham, t/v-1; Joey Casavano, cl or as-2; George Kelly, ts-3; Richard Wyands, p; Victor Gaskin, sb; Ronnie Cole, d.

Eisner & Lubin Auditorium, New York University, New York City.	
	12 December 1985
Three Little Words -2	Stash ST265

125

Mood Indigo -2, 3	Stash ST265
Sweet Lorraine -1	Stash ST265
Things Ain't What They Used To Be -2, 3	Stash ST265

Doc Cheatham is not present on *Sweet Georgia Brown* and *Body And Soul* from this session.

DOC CHEATHAM
Doc Cheatham, t; acc. Marcel Hendricks Combinatie: unknown instrumentation and personnel inc. Tom Baker, as/ts; Marcel Hendricks, p.

    Breda, Netherlands.   11 May 1986

        Please Don't Talk About Me When I'm Gone

                                    Jazz Crooner(Du)
                                      JC9811586

DOC CHEATHAM AND HIS SWEDISH JAZZ ALL STARS
Doc Cheatham, t/v; Staffan Arnberg, tb; Jan Åkerman, cl/as; Göran Eriksson, as; Claes Brodda, cl/ts; Henri Chaix, p; Mikael Selander, g-1; Olle Brostedt, g-2/sb-1; Göran Lind, sb-2; Sigge Dellert, d.

	Sandvik, Sweden	13 May 1987
870352-3	These Foolish Things -1	Kenneth(Sd) KS2061
870354-3	Miss Brown To You -1	Kenneth unissued
870355-2	The Man I Love -2	Kenneth(Sd) KS2061

Doc Cheatham, t/v; Göran Eriksson, as; Henri Chaix, p; Olle Brostedt, sb; Sigge Dellert, d.
    Same session.

870353-7	Nice Work If You Can Get It	Kenneth(Sd) KS2061

Doc Cheatham, t/v; Staffan Arnberg, tb-1; Jan Åkerman, cl-2/as-2; Göran Eriksson, as-3; Claes Brodda, cl-4/ts-4; Henri Chaix, p; Mikael Selander, g-5; Olle Brostedt, g-6/sb-5; Göran Lind, sb-6; Sigge Dellert, d.

	Sandvik, Sweden	14 May 1987
870356-4	I Wish I Had You -2, 4, 5	Kenneth(Sd) KS2061
870357-3	As Time Goes By -1, 2, 3, 4, 5	Kenneth unissued

870358-2	Sometimes I'm Happy -1, 2, 3, 4, 5	Kenneth unissued
870359-5	On The Sunny Side Of The Street -1, 2, 3, 4, 5	Kenneth(Sd) KS2061
870360-4	Moanin' Low -1, 2, 3, 4, 6	Kenneth(Sd) KS2061
870361-2	I Cried For You -1, 2, 3, 6	Kenneth(Sd) KS2061
870362-2	Body And Soul -1, 4, 6	Kenneth(Sd) KS2061

DOC CHEATHAM & SAMMY PRICE with LARS EDEGRAN'S JAZZ BAND

Doc Cheatham, t/v-1; Fred Lonzo, tb; Pud Brown, cl/ts; Sammy Price, p/v-2; Lars Edegran, g/a; Frank Fields, sb; Ernest Elly, d.

New Orleans, La.   23 April 1988

That Da-Da Strain	G.H.B. GHB249
I Can't Get Started -1	G.H.B. GHB249
I Can't Believe That You're In Love With Me	
	G.H.B. GHB249
Deed I Do	G.H.B. GHB249
Please Don't Talk About Me When I'm Gone -2	
	G.H.B. GHB249
Poor Butterfly	G.H.B. GHB249
Sweet Lorraine -1	G.H.B. GHB249
G.B. Boogie	G.H.B. GHB249
My Blue Heaven	G.H.B. GHB249

DOC CHEATHAM & HIS SWEDISH JAZZ ALL STARS

Doc Cheatham, t/v; Mikael Selander, g; Göran Lind, sb.

Stockholm, Sweden.   6 May 1988

880361-3	Confessin'	Kenneth(Sd) KS2062

Doc Cheatham, t/v; Staffan Arnberg, tb-1; Göran Eriksson, cl-2/as-2; Claes Brodda, cl-3/as-4/ts-5; Erik Persson, ts-6; Dick Cary, p-7/ah-8; Mikael Selander, g; Göran Lind, sb-9; Olle Brostedt, sb-10; Sigge Dellert, d.

Same session.

880362-3	A Kiss To Build A Dream On -1, 3, 5, 7, 9	Kenneth(Sd) KS2062
880363-1	I Double Dare You -1, 3, 4, 7, 9	Kenneth(Sd) KS2062
880364-3	Sweethearts On Parade -2, 8, 9	Kenneth(Sd) KS2062
880365-1	Once In A While -1, 2, 3, 7, 9	Kenneth(Sd) KS2062
880366-3	Our Monday Date -2, 3, 6, 7, 10	Kenneth(Sd) KS2062
880367-2	Dinah -2, 3, 4 , 5, 6, 7, 10	Kenneth(Sd) unissued

Doc Cheatham, t/v; Staffan Arnberg, tb-1; Göran Eriksson, cl-2/as-2; Claes Brodda, cl-3/as-4/ts-5; Erik Persson, ts-6; Dick Cary, p; Mikael Selander, g; Olle Brostedt, g-7/sb-8; Sigge Dellert, d-9.

Stockholm, Sweden.   7 May 1988

880368-2	I Guess I'll Get The Papers And Go Home -2, 7, 9	
		Kenneth(Sd) unissued
880369-4	Drop Me Off In Harlem -2, 7, 9	Kenneth(Sd) unissued
880370-3	I'm In The Mood For Love -1, 2, 4, 6, 8, 9	Kenneth(Sd) KS2062
880371-1	Jeepers Creepers -1, 2, 4, 6, 8, 9	Kenneth(Sd) KS2062
880372-4	Swing That Music -1, 2, 4, 6, 7, 9	Kenneth(Sd) KS2062
880373-3	Save It Pretty Mama -1, 2, 3, 5, 6, 7, 9	Kenneth(Sd) KS2062
880374-3	For All We Know -6, 8	Kenneth(Sd) unissued
880375-	Swing Down In New Orleans -1, 3, 6. 8	Kenneth(Sd) unissued

The unissued titles were scheduled for Kenneth KS2063, which was not issued.

DOC CHEATHAM

Doc Cheatham, t; Kenny Drew, p; Jimmy Woode, sb; Idris Muhammad, d.
Paris, France.   30/31 August 1988

I Only Have Eyes For You	Orange Blue(F) OB005(CD)
There's No You	Orange Blue(F) OB005(CD)
Dinah	Orange Blue(F) OB005(CD)
It's The Little Things That Mean So Much	Orange Blue(F) OB005(CD)
Jada	Orange Blue(F) OB005(CD)
I Double Dare You	Orange Blue(F) OB005(CD)
I'm In The Market For You	Orange Blue(F) OB005(CD)
Rump Steak Serenade	Orange Blue(F) OB005(CD)
That's My Home	Orange Blue(F) OB005(CD)
Drop Me Off In Harlem	Orange Blue(F) OB005(CD)
Where Are You?	Orange Blue(F) OB005(CD)
New Orleans	Orange Blue(F) OB005(CD)

MILT HINTON

Doc Cheatham, t; Eddie Barefield, as/ts; Buddy Tate, ts; Red Richards, p; Al
Casey, g; Milt Hinton, sb; Gus Johnson, d; Cab Calloway, v-1.
Englewood Cliffs, N.J.   6 March 1990

Good Time Charlie -1	Chiaroscuro CR(D)310 (CD)
The Yellow Front	Chiaroscuro CR(D)310 (CD)
Bloody Mary	Chiaroscuro CR(D)310 (CD)

DIZZY GILLESPIE
Dizzy Gillespie, Jon Faddis, Doc Cheatham, t; Junior Mance, p; Peter Washington, b; Kenny Washington, d.

Blue Note Club, New York City.	29-31 January 1992
Mood Indigo	Telarc CD83307 (CD)

DOC CHEATHAM with ROSEMARY GALLOWAY'S SWING SISTERS
Doc Cheatham, t/v-1; Sarah McElcheran, t; Jane Fair, cl/ts; Jim Galloway, ss/bar; Norman Amadio, p; Rosemary Galloway, sb/v-2; Don Vickery, d.

Toronto, Canada.	29 March 1992
Smokey Mary	Sackville(Ca) SKCD2-2038 (CD)
You're A Sweetheart	Sackville(Ca) SKCD2-2038 (CD)
Two Time Man -1	Sackville(Ca) SKCD2-2038 (CD)
A Shine On Your Shoes	Sackville(Ca) SKCD2-2038 (CD)
Judy	Sackville(Ca) SKCD2-2038 (CD)
Baby It's Cold Outside -1, 2	Sackville(Ca) SKCD2-2038 (CD)

ECHOES OF NEW ORLEANS
Doc Cheatham, t/v; Jerry Zigmont, tb; Sammy Rimington, cl/as; Jon Marks, p; Arvell Shaw, sb/v; John Russell, d.

Sweet Basil, New York City.	18 April 1992
Clarinet Marmalade	Big Easy CD005 (CD)
Three Little Words	Big Easy CD005 (CD)
Gee Baby Ain't I Good To You	Big Easy CD005 (CD)
My Buddy	Big Easy CD005 (CD)
Pennies From Heaven	Big Easy CD005 (CD)

Should I	Big Easy CD005 (CD)
Wabash Blues	Big Easy CD005 (CD)
Sweethearts On Parade	Big Easy CD005 (CD)
I Want To Be Happy	Big Easy CD005 (CD)
Ain't Misbehavin'	Big Easy CD005 (CD)
A Kiss To Build A Dream On	Big Easy CD005 (CD)
Them There Eyes	Big Easy CD005 (CD)
All Of Me	Big Easy CD005 (CD)
Struttin' With Some Barbecue	Big Easy CD005 (CD)

DOC CHEATHAM & HIS NEW YORK QUARTET

Doc Cheatham, t/v; Chuck Folds, p; Bucky Calabrese, sb; Jackie Williams, d.

New York City.	17/18 September 1992
That's My Home	Columbia CK53215 (CD)
Okay, Baby	Columbia CK53215 (CD)
Love You Madly	Columbia CK53215 (CD)
Blues In My Heart	Columbia CK53215 (CD)
Sleep	Columbia CK53215 (CD)
New Orleans	Columbia CK53215 (CD)
Muskrat Ramble	Columbia CK53215 (CD)

Was It A Dream?	Columbia CK53215 (CD)
Wolverine Blues	Columbia CK53215 (CD)
'Round Midnight	Columbia CK53215 (CD)
Miss Brown To You	Columbia CK53215 (CD)
Have You Met Miss Jones?	Columbia CK53215 (CD)
My Buddy	Columbia CK53215 (CD)
I Guess I'll Get The Papers And Go Home	Columbia CK53215 (CD)

DOC CHEATHAM
Doc Cheatham, t/v; Brian O'Connell, cl-1; Butch Thompson, p; Les Muscutt, g or bj-2; Billy Huntingdon, g-3/sb-2; Peter Badie, sb-3; Ernest Elly, d-4.
New Orleans   1994

Swinging Down In New Orleans -1, 2, 4	Jazzology JCD233 (CD)
When I Grow Too Old To Dream -1, 3	Jazzology JCD233 (CD)
I Want A Little Girl -1, 3	Jazzology JCD233 (CD)
You're Lucky To Me -1, 3	Jazzology JCD233 (CD)
Never Swat A Fly -1, 3	Jazzology JCD233 (CD)
I Can't Believe That You're In Love With Me-1, 3	Jazzology JCD233 (CD)
Memories Of You -1, 2, 4	Jazzology JCD233 (CD)
Avalon -1, 2	Jazzology JCD233 (CD)
Love Will Find A Way	Jazzology JCD233 (CD)

DOC CHEATHAM AND BUTCH THOMPSON
Doc Cheatham, t/v; Butch Thompson, p.

Carlisle, Mass.   April 1994

I've Got It Bad And That Ain't Good	Daring 3012 (CD)
If I Could Be With You One Hour Tonight	Daring 3012 (CD)
Rosetta	Daring 3012 (CD)
I Can't Get Started	Daring 3012 (CD)
Take The A Train	Daring 3012 (CD)
I'll Never Be The Same	Daring 3012 (CD)
If Your Dreams Come True	Daring 3012 (CD)
Georgia On My Mind	Daring 3012 (CD)
Too Much	Daring 3012 (CD)
Tin Roof Blues	Daring 3012 (CD)
I've Got A Crush On You	Daring 3012 (CD)

RED RICHARDS/GEORGE KELLY SEXTET
Doc Cheatham, t/v; Ole 'Fessor' Lindgreen, tb; George Kelly ts; Red Richards, p/v; Al Casey, g; Jan 'Big Bass' Jankeje, sb; Imre Köszegi, d.

Oberursel, Germany.   2 October 1994

Groove Move	Jazzpoint(G) CDJP1045 (CD)
I Wanna Little Girl Like Mama	Jazzpoint(G) CDJP1045 (CD)
Right On	Jazzpoint(G) CDJP1045 (CD)
Village Of Love	Jazzpoint(G) CDJP1045 (CD)
Up Stream	Jazzpoint(G) CDJP1045 (CD)
Idaho	Jazzpoint(G) CDJP1045 (CD)
Stella By Starlight	Jazzpoint(G) CDJP1045 (CD)
Sunday	Jazzpoint(G) CDJP1045 (CD)
It's A Little Thing That Means So Much	Jazzpoint(G) CDJP1045 (CD)

133

Strike Up The Band	Jazzpoint(G)
	CDJP1045 (CD)
Sweet Sue—Just You	Jazzpoint(G)
	CDJP1045 (CD)
Lady Be Good	Jazzpoint(G)
	CDJP1045 (CD)

INDEX TO DOC CHEATHAM ALBUMS (LP & CD)

Reissue Guide to pre-1953 recordings

Session	Label & Number	Album Title
c. Jun 26	King Jazz (It) KJ182	Ma Rainey: Complete Collection, Vol.3, 1926/27
Jul 29	Jazz-Time(F) 252.714-2	Black Jazz In Europe 1926-1930
Oct 29 (3 tracks)	Pathé 1727.261 (LP)	Black Bands In Paris 1929-1930
Oct 29 (3 tracks)	Jazz-Time(F) 251.716-2	Americans In Paris Vol. 1 1918-1935
8 Sep 31 (orig. takes)	Classics(F) 649	McKinney's Cotton Pickers 1930-1931
8 Sep 31 (alt. takes)	King Jazz(It) KJ124	McKinney's Cotton Pickers Great Alternatives 1928-31
10 Dec 36	Rarities(Da) 34 (LP)	Putney Dandridge Volume 3
11 Dec 39/18 Jan 40	Classics(F) 620	Teddy Wilson And His Orchestra 1939-1941
1 Apr 41	Classics(F) 631	Benny Carter And His Orchestra 1940-1941
19 Feb/26 Feb/11 Mar 44	Mosaic MR23-128 (LPs)	The Complete Commodore Jazz Recordings, Vol.II
(orig. takes only)	Commodore CCD7010	Jazz At Cafe Society, New York In The 40s.
25 Mar/1 Apr 44	Mosaic MR20-134(LPs)	The Complete Commodore Jazz Recordings, Vol.III
(orig. takes only)	Commodore CCD7001	Billie Holiday: Lady Day
(25 Mar 44; some alts)	Commodore(G) 8.24055	Billie Holiday: Fine And Mellow
(1 Apr 44; some alts)	Commodore(G) 8.24291	Billie Holiday: I'll Be Seeing You
20 Oct 44	Harlequin(E) HQCD19	Una Mae Carlisle 1944
27 Jun 45	Prestige PR7584 (LP)	Walter 'Foots' Thomas All Stars
31 Jan 50	Jazz Time(F) 789.327-2	Americans In Paris Vol. 6 (1942-1950)
1953	Black Lion BLCD760909	Pee Wee Russell: We're In The Money

Index to LPs and CDs Noted
(excluding discs included in the reissue guide above)

V.A. signifies 'Various Artists'; where no album title is given, this information has not been available.

Label & Number	Album Title	Session(s)
360° Music 2001	Beaver Harris: From Ragtime To No Time	20 Jan & 11 Feb 75
400 W.150 VLP400	Clyde Bernhardt: More Blues And Jazz From Harlem	10/20 Nov 73
Atlantic SD1219	Wilbur De Paris: New New Orleans Jazz	2 Apr 55
Atlantic SD1288	Wilbur De Paris Plays Cole Porter	25 Feb 57
Atlantic SD1300	Wilbur De Paris: Something Old, New, Gay, Blue	26 May & 15 Dec 58
Atlantic SD1318	Wilbur De Paris: That's A Plenty	20 Apr 59
Atlantic SD1336	Wilbur De Paris: The Wild Jazz Age	9 May 60
Atlantic SD1343	Herbie Mann: Afro Jazz 6 & 4 Trumpets	2/3 Aug 60
Atlantic SD1363	Wilbur De Paris On The Riviera	10 Jul 60
Atlantic SD1552	Wilbur De Paris: Over & Over Again	8 Apr 59 & 16/17 Nov 60
Atlantic SD8804	Jay McShann: The Big Apple Bash	3/8/10 Aug 78
Barron VLP401	Clyde Bernhardt: Sittin' On Top Of The World	16 Sep & 9 Oct 75
Barron VLP403	Harlem Blues & Jazz Band 1973-1980	20 Nov 73
Big Easy CD005	Echoes Of New Orleans: Live At Sweet Basil	18 Apr 92
Black & Blue 33.079	Sammy Price: Fire	1 May 75
Black & Blue 33.090	Doc Cheatham: Hey Doc!	2 May 75
Black & Blue 33.103	Carrie Smith: Do Your Duty	26 Jul 76
Black & Blue 33.159	Harlem On Parade	19 Jul 77
Black & Blue 33.560	Sammy Price: Rockin' Boogie	12 May 75
Black & Blue 59.080-2	V.A.: Explosive Drums	21 May 75
Black & Blue 59.090-2	Doc Cheatham: Hey Doc!	2/21 May 75
Black & Blue 233.079	Sammy Price: Fire	1/20/21 May 75
Black & Blue 233.119	Carrie Smith: Nobody Knows You When You're Down And Out	26 Jul 76
Black Lion BLP30190	Earl Hines: Swingin' Away	5/7 Dec 73

Blues Blood BB132	Jim Bartow	c.1975
Chiaroscuro CR132	Buck Clayton Jam Session Vol. 1	25/26 Mar 74
Chiaroscuro CR163	Buck Clayton Jam Session Vol. 4	25/26 Mar 74
Chiaroscuro CR(D)310	Milt Hinton: Old Man Time	6 Mar 90
Club Français Du Disque 142	Sammy Price: Les Grands Succes De Gershwin	Oct 58
Columbia CK53215	The Eighty-Seven Years Of Doc Cheatham	17/18 Sep 92
Columbia CL1098	V.A.: The Sound Of Jazz	5 Dec 57
Columbia CL1152	The Jazz Odyssey Of James Rushing, Esq.	26/27 Feb 58
Commodore XFL14428	Billie Holiday: Fine And Mellow	25 Mar 44
Commodore XFL15351	Billie Holiday: I'll Be Seeing You	1 Apr 44
Counterpoint CH564	Juanita Hall Sings The Blues	1958
CTJC SLP8	V.A.:	18 Mar 72
CTJC SLP12	V.A.:	25 Oct 75 & 24 Jan 76
CTJC CLP17	V.A.:	c. 1980
CTJC CLP19	V.A.:	20 Nov82
Daring 3012	Doc Cheatham & Butch Thompson: Butch & Doc	Apr 94
Everest FS310	Billie Holiday	8 Dec 57
Extreme Rarities 1002	V.A.: Hot Jazz On Film	8 Dec 57
G.H.B. GHB84	Natalie Lamb-Sammy Price And The Blues	c. 1979
G.H.B. GHB249	Doc Cheatham & Sammy Price In New Orleans	23 Apr 88
Harlequin HQ2026	V.A.: Jazz And Hot Dance In Spain	Jul 29
Jazz Crooner JC13684	V.A.: 14th International Jazz Festival, Breda, 1984	2/3 Jun 84
Jazz Crooner JC283181	V.A.: International Jazz Festival, Breda	May 81
Jazz Crooner JC9811586	V.A.: 16th International Jazz Festival, Breda, 1986	11 May 86
Jazz Ways 106/2	Doc Cheatham: Doc Prescribes	Dec 73
Jazzology JCD233	Doc Cheatham: Swinging Down In New Orleans	1994
Jazzpoint CDJP1045	Red Richards/George Kelly: Groove Move	2 Oct 94
Jezebel JZ102 (2xLP)	Adolphus "Doc" Cheatham	4/5/9 Apr 73
Kenneth KS2061	Doc Cheatham: A Tribute To Billie Holiday	13/14 May 87
Kenneth KS2062	Doc Cheatham: A Tribute To Louis Armstrong	6/7 May 88

Mahogany 558.103	Doc Cheatham: Jive At Five	22 Jul 75
Metronome MELP627	Fessor's Nighthawks: John—Doc & Herb	20 Aug 79
Music Minus One 4090/3	Dick Wellstood: From Dixie To Swing	c. 1972
Musicmasters 5047-2-C	Benny Goodman: Live At The Rainbow Grill	3/4 Jun 66
New York Jazz J002	Doc Cheatham: Too Marvelous For Words	25/26 Oct 82
New York Jazz J003	Doc Cheatham: I've Got A Crush On You	25/26 Oct 82
Old School Band 03	Old School Band: 25 Ans	14 Oct 83
Ombrads 2903	Benny Goodman	19 May 66
Orange Blue OB005	Doc Cheatham: Dear Doc	30/31 Aug 88
Parkwood PW101	Doc Cheatham: It's A Good Life	6/7 Dec 82
Parkwood PW104	The Fabulous Doc Cheatham	16/17 Nov 83
Parkwood PW106	The Authentic Art Hodes Rhythm Section	7/8 Jun 85
Pumpkin 116	V.A.: The Real Sound Of Jazz	8 Dec 57
RCA 430.272	McKinney's Cotton Pickers	8 Sep 31
RCA 741.073	Benny Carter And His Orchestra	1 Apr 41
RCA FXM1-7059	McKinney's Cotton Pickers, Vol. 5	8 Sep 31
RCA LPL1-5030	Jane Harvey	20 Feb 74
RCA LPL1-5031	V.A.: Swing Today Vol. 1	20 Feb 74
RCA LFL1-5032	V.A.: Swing Today Vol. 2	15 Feb 74
RCA LFL1-5034	Buddy Tate & Earle Warren: The Count's Men	12 Jul 73
RCA LFL1-5036	Vic Dickenson	15 Feb 74
RCA LFL1-5067	V.A.: Swing Today Vol. 3	12 Jul 73
RCA-Victor LPMS3762	Introducing Cap'n John Handy	15/16/17/18 Nov 66
Sackville 3013	Doc Cheatham & Sammy Price: Doc And Sammy	17 Nov 76
Sackville 3029	Doc Cheatham & Sammy Price: Black Beauty	31 Oct 79
Sackville CD2-3045	Doc Cheatham: At The Bern Jazz Festival	30 Apr 83, 17 May 84, 5 Jan 85
Sackville SKCD2-2038	Doc Cheatham: You're A Sweetheart	29 Mar 92
Stash ST254	Highlights In Jazz Anniversary Concert	Feb 85
Stash ST265	Doc Cheatham & George Kelly: Echoes Of Harlem	12 Dec 85
Storyville STLP307	Mahogany Hall All Stars	1953
Storyville STLP308	Pee Wee Russell And The Mahogany Hall All Stars	1953

Storyville STCD5010	Buddy Tate: Jive At Five	22 Jul 75
Sultra SU2-1006	Lionel Hampton: 50th Anniversary Album	1 Jul 78
Swing SW8410	V.A.: Eartha Kitt-Doc Cheatham-Bill Coleman	
		31 Jan 50
Swingville SVLP2021	Harold Baker & Doc Cheatham: Shorty And Doc	
		17 Jan 61
Swingville SVLP2031	Leonard Gaskin: At The Jazz Band Ball	30 Nov 61
Tax M8018	Teddy Wilson And His Big Band 1939-1940	11 Dec 39
Telarc CD83307	Dizzy Gillespie: To Diz With Love	29-31 Jan 92
Timeless SJP142	Lionel Hampton All Star Band At Newport '78	
		2 Jul 78
Verve MGV8392	Herbie Mann: Flute, Brass, Vibes & Percussion	1960

Index

Index

Index

Index

Index